P9-CRM-131

An American Beach for African Americans

University Press of Florida

GAINESVILLE TALLAHASSEE TAMPA BOCA RATON PENSACOLA ORLANDO MIAMI JACKSONVILLE

An American Beach for African Americans

MARSHA DEAN PHELTS

Copyright 1997 by the Board of Regents of the State of Florida
Printed in the United States of America on acid-free paper
All rights reserved

02 01 00 99 98 97 6 5 4 3 2 1

Library of Congress Cataloging-in-Publication Data
Phelts, Marsha Dean.
An American Beach for African Americans / Marsha Dean Phelts.
   p. cm.
Includes bibliographical references.
ISBN 0-8130-1504-9 (alk. paper)
1. American Beach (Fla.)—History. 2. Afro-Americans—Florida—
American Beach—History. I. Title.
F319.A45P47 1997
975.9'11—dc21 97-7277

The University Press of Florida is the scholarly publishing agency for the State University
System of Florida, comprised of Florida A & M University, Florida Atlantic University,
Florida International University, Florida State University, University of Central Florida,
University of Florida, University of North Florida, University of South Florida, and
University of West Florida.

University Press of Florida
15 Northwest 15th Street
Gainesville, FL 32611

To Alice Wanzer Grant, a master teacher.
Without her tutelage this story would not be.

Contents

Preface

This book is the story of four overlapping eras in the history of an enclave now known as American Beach, a 200-acre coastal community of African Americans on the southern end of Amelia Island in the northeast corner of Florida. The first period, from 1796 to 1865—the time from slavery to freedom—includes the stories of the pioneering families, some of whose descendants still live in the area. During the second era, the Jim Crow period, the law denied beach access to citizens of color. This exclusion led the founders of American Beach to form the small resort community during the segregated days of the Great Depression. In the third era this recreational group began to shape itself into a culturally focused, family-oriented resort community. The fourth era has been dominated by the threat posed by conglomerate resort developers to this historic barrier island African American community.

If you have never visited the community, you have a treat in store, and I hope you will add your voice to ours to guarantee that there will always be an American Beach. Florida's coast features many high-rise condominiums and resort communities. Building one more would not do much to improve our quality of life. But to add another on the site now occupied by American Beach would be tragic indeed, because it would rob future generations of the opportunity to experience one of the many cultures that make up our diverse national community.

American Beach. There is no other place like it on the American landscape.

〰〰〰〰〰〰 Hundreds of people have helped me gather information I have put to use to write this book. I thank those who helped me compile this story. I thank our ancestors for the legacy of faith and accomplishment they passed to us.

I especially wish to acknowledge these individuals: my tutor and master teacher, Alice Grant, and my friend, Corrine Brown, for reading my pamphlet-sized manuscript in 1992 and telling me that a more extensive story needed to be told; David Nolan, who has been my mentor since I first read his endearing book about the Florida land boom, *Fifty Feet in Paradise,* for coaching me and guiding me to the references I needed; Kevin McCarthy, another master teacher, for being there; Howard Denson of Florida Community College in Jacksonville and the exceptional services he provided through Intelligent Eye, Inc., by proofreading the manuscript and eliminating many errors; Marion Graham, for turning me loose in a warehouse of records and canceled checks from the Afro-American Life Insurance Company that he thought too important to throw away; and Ernestine Latson Smith, for readily sharing with me keepsakes from her family archives.

Archivists throughout the state made available legal records that provided backup documentation for each personal interview I conducted. I especially thank T. J. Greeson, Clerk of Courts, Nassau County, where I spent five summers reading deed and record books; Henry Cook, Clerk of City and Duval County Courts, and Margaret Walters, who believe it is their job to help citizens gain access to the records in their charge; Carol Harris and Arden Brugger in the Florida/Genealogy Collection and Mary Ann Pearson and Beverly Spicer in the Periodicals and Business Collection of the Jacksonville Public Library.

I am also grateful to Dwight Wilson, Jack Pate, and Jean McCormick for the years of recording and collecting data of the Beaches Area Historical Society and for sharing so freely; Joan Morris and Jody Norman, curators of the Photograph Collection at the Florida State Archives, Tallahassee, for providing pictures and stories beyond a genie's wish to illustrate the trail that led to American Beach; Robert Crews at Reddi Arts for helping me at a moment's notice with my pictures; Byron Brown, for helping to find the deeds that unraveled years of hearsay into facts on the Harrison/American Beach property; and a friend from childhood, Rodney Hurst, for spinning his priceless collection of soulful beach melodies from the 1950s and the 1960s and helping me to re-create the mood that prevailed during the American Beach boom; Sayre Sheldon, Canter Brown, Elaine Adams, Ruth Waters, Kara Mort, and Gregory Hanson, for their invaluable support and the cheers they gave; Jim Nordman, for rescuing my damaged disk four days before the manuscript deadline, and for preserving my inner peace and sanity; Charlotte Dwight Stewart, Camilla Perkins Thompson, and Maxine Ray, who wrote weekly columns for the *Florida Star, Jacksonville Free Press,* and *Fernandina News-Leader,* for inspiring me to bring this project to fruition. Their articles through the years about our local cultural legacy have been inspirational. I thank Mary and Ericka Simpson, Rita and Sylvia Perry, and Ike and Harriet Williams for the trove of resources they made available to me.

So much thanks goes to my husband, Mike, my mama, Eva, and my aunt Pearlie for understanding my passionate obsession to complete this saga. Once I started on this journey, they never admonished me to slow down or abandon this project as it consumed my complete attention.

I also thank the staff of the University Press of Florida, especially Alexandra Leader and Walda Metcalf, who made my dream come true. I am grateful to them for their patience and direction, and to Skip Rothstein for sending me to them.

Thanks be to God.

An African American Beach

The blood that unites us is thicker than the water that divides us.
NELSON MANDELA TO RANDALL ROBINSON

Florida has the longest coastline in the contiguous United States, with 1,197 miles of shoreline running from Amelia Island on the northeast Atlantic coast to Gulf Beach on the Gulf of Mexico in the northwest. Much of this shore has long been publicly owned, but for a hundred years after the abolition of slavery, laws usually forbade African Americans to enjoy the beaches.

Until 1884 blacks who wanted to visit one of six public beaches in the Jacksonville area had to stay home. That year the southern end of Pablo Beach (later Jacksonville Beach) was opened to blacks one day a week. During the first three decades of the 1900s, Manhattan Beach, near Mayport, became a popular black resort.

The excursions to Pablo Beach, organized by black civic and religious groups, congregated around a wonderful facility called the Coney Island pavilion. The outings drew huge crowds. The *Pablo Beach Breeze* reported on June 2, 1888, "The colored excursion last Monday was a jumbo affair; there being between six and seven hundred of Jacksonville's colored population on the beach during the day."

Hundreds of beachgoers and vacationers gathered on American Beach during the annual outing of the Afro-American Life Insurance Company in 1937. The pavilion is perched on a dune. Courtesy Saramae Stewart Richardson.

Coney Island, ca. 1900. This round yellow wood pavilion on Pablo Beach (right) survived from the 1880s until it was demolished in 1926. Blacks could use the beach and this facility on Mondays only. Courtesy Beaches Area Historical Society, Jacksonville Beach.

Sunday baptism services for a black congregation on Pablo Beach near Fifth Avenue South, 1934. White beachgoers are observing from a seawall. Courtesy Jean Hayden McCormick, Beaches Area Historical Society, Jacksonville Beach.

By prearrangement, on certain Sundays black church congregations could also hold baptisms in the ocean. Immediately afterward, the worshipers were required to return to their churches to conclude their services.[1]

MANHATTAN BEACH

Manhattan Beach, the first beach community in northeast Florida created as a recreational resort for blacks, got its start when industrialist Henry Flagler's Florida East Coast Railway sold some beachfront property to black railroad workers in the early 1900s. Located near Mayport, a Jacksonville fishing community on the southern shore of the St. Johns River, Manhattan Beach was originally part of the DeWees Land Grant, 2,290 acres granted Andrew DeWees in 1790 by the king of Spain.

As Flagler's rail lines had crisscrossed Florida's east coast, he had established railroad villages and sold excess property to developers, who built communities around the station stops. In 1899, Flagler built a line from

Jacksonville to Pablo Beach, and in 1900 extended it to the northeastern end of Mayport, running it through a large tract of the DeWees Grant.

Among the first blacks to buy property on Manhattan Beach were W. S. and Louise Stephenson, Ella Harris, and Capitola Washington.[2] Other well-known property owners included the Mack Wilsons of Jacksonville and the William Middletons of Fernandina, who operated pavilions that gave Manhattan Beach the flavor of a little New York City. At one of them, Little Coney Island, resort goers found an amusement park for children with a merry-go-round and swings. Some of the streets of Manhattan Beach bore the names of presidents and patriots: Washington, Lincoln, Roosevelt, Jefferson. Others were named after local statesmen, such as Isaiah D. Hart, founder of Jacksonville, and Joseph E. Lee, one of Florida's first black lawyers.

Among the parishes of black churches, the beach became popular for summer excursions, and by 1905 blacks were descending on Manhattan Beach by the trainload. Many times I sat on Big Mama Agnes Cobb's front porch shelling black-eyed peas, listening to her tell of the long-ago junkets that she, Grandpapa Randall, and their six children—my aunts and uncles—relished on Manhattan Beach. From Jacksonville, the forty-four-mile round-

Mack Wilson's pavilion, ca. 1927. The pavilion operated day and night on Manhattan Beach, providing entertainment, dining, lodging, and bathing facilities. Courtesy Eartha White Collection, University of North Florida Library, Jacksonville.

My grandmother, Big Mama, Agnes Lloyd Cobb, 1925, who enthralled her grandchildren with tales of excursions to Manhattan Beach. Courtesy Eva C. Lamar.

trip cost adults sixty cents. I had trouble believing Big Mama when she said that on these trains, which left very early in the morning and returned home at dark, black people rode in the front cars and whites rode in the cars at the end—until my mama explained that the soot, cinders, and smoke from the train's engine blew back and settled heaviest on the cars closest to the engine. Before the train reached the beach, according to Aunt Annie Bell, everyone's clean clothes were covered with soot. Aunt Pearlie remembered that the children wore their swimsuits under their clothes. After swimming, they showered in what they called a mule stall—an outdoor shower—played until their swimsuits dried, then put their clothes back on.

One special day, Big Mama packed up all the youngsters except Vera, the youngest, and sent them to the beach with their papa, who could keep an eye on them while he worked at his subcontracting job, hauling sand to

Surprise birthday party for Eva Lamar on July 29, 1990, at her home on the end of the American Beach. Left to right: the Cobb sisters, Pearlie Scarborough, Vera Gibson, Mama, Eva Lamar, and Annie Bell Nelson. Courtesy Bob Self.

build A1A, the road that runs the length of Florida's Atlantic coast. Big Mama packed a basket lunch with meat, biscuits, figs, tea cakes, and water, and cautioned the children not to go in the ocean. Not only did they have the treat of playing in the sand on top of the dunes, building sand castles, and digging their feet down into the cool beach sand, they also had the thrill of watching their papa at his exciting job, which required—mules!

My grandfather hired his teenage son, my uncle Willie, as a mule driver for his sand-hauling operation. To move dirt from the dunes, two mules pulled a drag pan or slip pan, which scooped the dirt up like a huge shovel. Once the pan was filled and dragged to its destination, the slip pan man, who needed to be enormously strong, would lift it by its two handles and empty it. Three-mule wheeler teams moved bigger loads; upon reaching the dump site, a mule instead of a man dragged the pan to tilt it over. Willie earned $3.00 a day, just like the grown men. Half of that went to Big Mama. Every Sunday, when the other workers had the day off, Willie and his younger brother Freddie took the train to the beach to water and feed the mules—and to catch a mess of jumbo crabs. The rest of the family awaited their return, with a big pot of seasoned water heated and ready for a Sunday evening crab boil. One Sunday the boys arrived home empty-handed. Freddie had fallen asleep on the train coming back to town, and the crabs escaped from their crocus sack and scurried all over the car. Whose crabs were they? the conductor wanted to know. Willie, sensing danger, kept mum. Awakened by the commotion, Freddie too had the sense to keep

William Middleton's Manhattan Beach pavilion and boardwalk, a comfort station for beachgoers, ca. 1920. Courtesy Eartha White Collection, University of North Florida Library, Jacksonville.

Church groups flocked to Manhattan Beach, as seen here in this mix of friends from Florida and Georgia. Front row, left to right: Gwendolyn Leapheart, Nettye Leapheart, Dorothy Waites. Back row, left to right: unidentified man, Rev. D. G. Woods, Irene Glover, Mrs. James Waites. Courtesy Gwendolyn Leapheart.

Left: Rachel Austin, secretary for the Knights of Pythias, and postal worker F. Henry Williams having fun in their fashionable bathing attire at a Manhattan Beach outing sponsored by the Knights. Courtesy Gwendolyn Leapheart.

Below: When trains stopped running to Mayport in 1932, beachgoers piled into cars and buses to reach Manhattan Beach. Courtesy Eartha White Collection, University of North Florida Library, Jacksonville.

quiet. At the station, they simply got off the train without the crocus sack, jumped on the bicycle they shared, and rode home.

For a quarter of a century Manhattan Beach was a Mecca for black beach day-trip excursions, but in the Depression year of 1932 the Mayport/Manhattan Beach railroad line stopped running.[3] People came to the beach by car, truck, and church bus, but in fewer numbers. A few seasons later severe erosion threatened the beach's existence; the Atlantic was swallowing up oceanfront lots. After a mysterious fire destroyed Mack Wilson's pavilion, the last public facility on Manhattan Beach, in 1938, fewer and fewer blacks came.[4] Old-timers say that the fire was purposely set to drive blacks off the beach because it was now too close to the white beach communities creeping south from the northern end of Duval County.

When the federal government appropriated part of the beach to construct the Mayport Naval Base during World War II, Manhattan Beach disappeared except as a joyous memory.

Butler's Beach

As Manhattan Beach declined as a seaside recreation site for blacks, two other African American oceanfront developments got under way—Butler Beach near St. Augustine and American Beach on Amelia Island. In the mid-1920s, a group of blacks in St. Augustine who wanted to buy oceanfront property there could find no one willing to sell to them. As was the case in much of the South, the whites in the area had long refused to sell land to blacks. Finally, however, a series of events brought these black buyers together with Edgar Pomar, who had homesteaded seventy-eight acres of ocean and riverfront property on Anastasia Island, ten miles south of St. Augustine in St. Johns County, between the ocean and the Matanzas River. By 1926 the Florida land-boom hype had died down; that same year Pomar's wife died and the area was devastated by a hurricane. At that point Pomar, who had given up on his plan to develop his property, didn't care what color the buyers were.

Frank B. Butler seized the opportunity. A real estate broker, grocer, civic leader, and ardent church worker, Butler formed a corporation that purchased the tract and developed it as an African American seaside resort. Through the remainder of the Jim Crow years, Butler's Beach served as a

Frank B. Butler, founder of Butler Beach, in his College Park Realty office in St. Augustine ca. 1927. Courtesy Florida State Archives.

haven for blacks. Lots were sold and homes built. At one point in the 1950s eleven businesses operated in this island community.[5]

Today, two parks are named in honor of the beach's founder, Butler's Beach Park on the ocean and Frank B. Butler County Park on the Matanzas River. Butler's grandson, Rudolph Hadley, lives with his wife, Joyce, in an ocean-front home filled with history. The house started life as a motel, where the Reverends Martin Luther King Jr., Andrew Young, Ralph Abernathy, and C. T. Vivian stayed during the 1964 civil rights demonstrations in St. Augustine.

On the river side near the Frank B. Butler County Park lives Otis Mason, the only African American ever elected superintendent of schools in St. Johns County. Apart from Hadley and Mason, the residents of this beach community are white. Butler sold much of his beach property to the state of Florida in 1958 for use as a state park. Through the years, other black property owners sold to private interests. The Butler name and the streets named after members of Butler's family are the only reminders that the beach and riverfront park were developed by African Americans during the days of segregation.

In 1935, during the formative years of Butler's Beach, the Pension Bureau of the Afro-American Life Insurance Company purchased and developed what came to be American Beach. The story begins with the rags-to-riches rise of the man who served as president and chairman of the board of the Afro beginning in 1919, Abraham Lincoln Lewis. Lewis came to Jacksonville with his impoverished family from Madison County, Florida, in 1876, when he was eleven. Through hard work, determination, and regular saving, he managed to amass a fortune and by his midfifties was top man at Afro.

Ruth Campbell Stewart, 100 years old at the time of our interview in 1993, recalled that Lewis and his wife, Mary, belonged to community organizations such as the Most Worshipful Grand Lodge, Inc., Heroines of Jericho, the Mt. Olive AME Church, and the Bethel Baptists Institutional Church, which sponsored those early day trips to Pablo and Manhattan Beaches. She remembers the Lewis home on Pablo Beach, on 120 S. Third Street,

The earliest known picture of American Beach, ca. 1935, before the first homes were constructed there. At the time, tents were common temporary beach shelters. Eartha White, pictured in the right foreground, sponsored annual picnics and outings to American Beach for children and the elderly. Courtesy Florida State Archives.

People parked their cars on American Beach from the beginning. The road leading to the beach was made of oyster shell and the access ramp was made of plank boards. Courtesy Ernestine Smith.

three streets from the ocean.[6] Lewis also owned a bungalow there, which he rented to Adam and Janie Jackson, and a small amount of property at south Pablo Beach where access to blacks was limited.[7]

When Lewis's insurance company began its search during the Depression for a total beach community for African Americans, his eye fell on Amelia Island in Nassau County, where hundreds of acres were available for resort development. Land was affordable, and it was a good time to buy real estate. Lewis and the Afro decided upon a large stretch of beach front near the southern tip of the island. It proved a sound investment. The American Beach community thrived.

Thirteen miles long, Amelia Island is a coveted 11,600-acre barrier island, the only location in the United States over which the flags of eight different nations have flown: the French, Spanish, English, and Patriots flags; the

Green Cross of Florida; and the flags of Mexico, the Confederacy, and the United States.[8] At its northern end today lies the city of Fernandina Beach. American Beach, once safely isolated, now struggles to maintain affordable life-styles while sandwiched between two colossal resorts, the Ritz Carlton-Summer Beach and the Amelia Island Plantation.

By nature's design, the island is a beautiful enclave. Motorists traveling the Buccaneer Trail along the Amelia Island Parkway, awed by the palatial Ritz Carlton Hotel and the wealthy Amelia Island Plantation communities, may find it hard to believe that Amelia Island's southern tip was once owned by blacks. But before 1970, a white face on the southeastern end of the island would have indeed been rare.

In 1992, the Florida legislature named the first of 141 sites that would comprise the Florida Black Heritage Trail—American Beach.

Aerial view of the downtown historic district of Fernandina Beach, 1989. Prominent features include the marina, the Nassau County Courthouse, and the post office. Courtesy Ed Mathews.

Franklin Town

We were all Black and we were all poor and we were all right there in place.
For us, the larger community didn't exist.
BARBARA JORDAN

American Beach was not the first black settlement to take root along the southeastern shores of Amelia Island. A self-sufficient community of African Americans had existed on the southern end of the island in Franklin Town since 1862, ex-slave families who had come there from the nearby Samuel Harrison plantation. Descendants of those families have lived continuously on those same shores ever since.

SLAVERY TIME TALK

Samuel Harrison, a planter from South Carolina, settled on southern Amelia Island during the English occupation in 1781. Fifteen years later, on July 5, 1796, he applied for a land grant for the property he had homesteaded. One of many land grants issued to Harrison and his sons, this one consisted of a 700-acre tract at the mouth of the Nassau River; it was deeded to him by the Spanish government, with his ownership later confirmed by the government of the United States.[1]

The Harrisons owned slaves on Amelia Island from 1781 until Union soldiers occupied Fernandina during the Civil War. Although the United States banned slave trading after 1808, Florida's wealthiest planter, Zephaniah Kingsley, ensconced on his Laurel Grove estate on the St. Johns River since 1803, continued importing slaves, earning considerable profit. The trading continued even after the United States acquired Florida in 1821.[2]

A sinister chapter in Fernandina's history opened in 1808, when the slave trade joined the town's other profitable smuggling enterprises. Because Florida was not a U.S. territory, the anti-importation law did not apply to Amelia Island. Instead, it made Fernandina, on the southern border of the United States, a lucrative trading site; slaves could conveniently be smuggled ashore from Africa and later sold throughout the South..

If a slave ship was stopped off the Florida coast, however, its captain was subject to the death penalty. Captains hard pressed by the U.S. Patrol dumped their human cargo overboard.[3] Ships who slipped past the patrol to the Fernandina port saved their owners' investment.

FORTY ACRES AND A MULE

During the Civil War, Fernandina was one of the first ports of the South to come under Union control; only then were the slaves on Amelia Island and the Harrison plantation freed. Gabriel Means, a former slave from the Harrison plantation, was among a vast number of black men who joined the U.S. Colored Infantry to fight with the Union in exchange for their freedom. Means enlisted on December 2, 1862, in Company A of the infantry's Thirty-third Regiment, where he served for three years.[4] Upon his return to Amelia Island after the war, he found that, as a result of recent legal action, much of his former owner's land had become U.S. government property available for homesteading.

To create a safe transition for the manumission of Negroes, Major General William T. Sherman had issued Special Field Order No. 15 from Savannah, Georgia, January 16, 1865, setting aside land for the settlement of Negro communities: "The islands from Charleston south, the abandoned rice fields along the rivers for thirty miles back from the sea, and the country bordering the St. Johns River, Florida, are reserved and set apart for the settlement of the Negroes now made free by the acts of war and the proclamation of the President of the United States."[5] Such laws as these, effected in few places outside Union-controlled states, enabled newly freed black

"Negroes in new blue coats and fine equipage," Civil War soldiers in Fernandina in a 1938 drawing by John Rae. In the background is the Florida House, built in 1857 by the Florida Railroad Company. It remains in operation today, providing, now as then, food, lodging, and spirits. Courtesy Florida State Archives.

families to homestead and cultivate land for themselves on property where they had once been slaves.

FRANKLIN TOWN'S PATRIARCHS AND DESCENDANTS

Franklin Town was named after a person, but not in the way you would think. In 1872 a former slave agreed to pay one Albert Cone $500.00 for four acres of riverfront property near Jacksonville. The former slave's name was Franklin E. Town. Cone never conveyed the deed to the property and Town never handed over the money, but the name stuck. Although Franklin E. Town never owned property there, Franklin Town kept his name.[6]

A number of African American families who remained on Amelia Island after emancipation became property owners and developed Franklin Town, where they eked out a living by farming, ranching, and fishing. By 1878, during the presidency of Rutherford B. Hayes, families headed by Gabriel Means, Stephen Drummond, Gilbert Hopkins, and Robert Stewart and their heirs had received title to their lands, not always as a result of land grants. Gabriel Means, the former slave of Robert Harrison, paid $340 for the forty acres he bought from Hope, Wendell P., and Ella Gifford in 1887—$8.50 an acre, when land in Nassau County and throughout Florida was selling for between fifty cents and $3.00 an acre.[7]

Gabriel Means's descendants, today my immediate neighbors on American Beach, have provided me with documents, deeds, letters, pension papers, and rich recollections of life on Amelia Island. Rosa Thomas and Evelyn Jefferson, granddaughter and great-granddaughter of Means, described his large two-story Franklin Town home with its wide wraparound porch; the fruit orchards, where their ancestors grew oranges, grapefruits, peaches, pomegranates, plums, watermelons, and figs; the pecan and walnut trees that provided a plentiful and profitable harvest.[8]

Farmer Flumer Hopkins outside his stable in Franklin Town, 1930. Hopkins was a descendant of Civil War veteran Gilbert Hopkins, among the recipients of Amelia Island land set aside for blacks. Courtesy Marie Thomas.

Lillie Means Ray (1909–1994), the historian for Franklin Town families, in her Fernandina Beach home in 1990. Her grandfather, Gabriel Means, a Civil War veteran, was a pioneer settler of Franklin Town. Courtesy Frances Lovett Alexander.

Franklin Town families also raised livestock for profit—cattle, hogs, chickens, turkeys, and geese. Descendants with whom I spoke remember Means's practice of tending the cattle. Alternating grazing locations to allow the grasses to replenish themselves, during the winter months he moved the herd to Little Talbot Island, and in the summer, to Big Talbot Island, the first two barrier islands south of Amelia. With the bridges that would connect these islands many years in the future, Means drove the cattle across Nassau Sound on horseback.

The dozen or so families who lived in Franklin Town owned huge acreages, with the ocean and the river as their east and west boundaries. From the cornfields came sweet kernels for grinding into grits and meal. In the "evening field" on the river side of the island, families planted sugarcane, rice, and sweet potatoes. Hitched to a long lever, Means's old gray mule, Mabel, trudged around the barrel filled with cane to grind it into juice, which was then poured into a big boiler and cooked down to syrup.[9]

The Means family historian and keeper of the records, Lillie Means Ray, told me of living in the Harrison homestead, and about her white and mulatto cousins from the Harrison side of the family. She helped me visualize American Beach when it was nothing but high hills blanketed with white sand, where sea oats anchored their roots at the edge of a pristine shore. And she advised me to talk with her cousins up the road in Stewartville, descendants of Robert Stewart, another former slave who had acquired property after the Civil War.

The Stewarts spoke of their ancestral home in Franklin Town, recalling that a great portion of their family income came from the sea. Their parents were Hayes and Josephine Hopkins Stewart. Hayes Stewart earned a good living for his family of fourteen children from fishing. Along with his sons, he seine fished and set out gill nets, bringing in trout that sold for twenty-five cents a pound in the market. They strung the fish that didn't sell at the market in sets of six and sold them for ten cents door-to-door across the island. Stewart's son Willie said that fish were so abundant that until the late 1950s, as soon as they walked out to spread the net in the river, fish bumped together in the rush to swim into them. Oyster beds at Walk-

A 1900 photograph of the Reverend Henry Harrison (1803–1917), son of planter E. Harrison and cousin of Eartha White, who prophesied at Eartha's Epiphany that she would be a storehouse to all the people. Courtesy Eartha White Collection, University of North Florida, Jacksonville.

Workers culling shrimp at Fernandina dock, 1957. Courtesy Florida State Archives.

ers Landing at the foot of the river supplied plenty of plump, succulent morsels for oyster roasts. The landing, where Franklin Town's boats were once launched for fishing expeditions, today is a popular Amelia Island Plantation Resort location for private parties and receptions. Here the southward-flowing Atlantic Intracoastal Waterway enters the sea to the east through Nassau Sound.

Shrimping has been a major industry on Amelia Island since the turn of the nineteenth century. Seamen from Franklin Town credit Portuguese shrimpers, "Porgie boys," for teaching them offshore shrimping. When the Portuguese sloops came ashore, black women picked and headed loads of shrimp for shipping by boat or trucks.[10] The bountiful catches enabled families in the new township to buy their homes and land and, in later years, to purchase automobiles.

Franklin Town became a self-sufficient community with its own school and church—an independent United Methodist Church built by Means on his land and principally by his labor. Means and his wife, Edie

Drummond, deeded a parcel of their property for the Franklin Town United Methodist Church in 1888.[11]

The church Means built survived for more than half a century. Means's grandchildren recalled with enthusiasm the church-sponsored picnics "more exciting than Christmas," when members of Fernandina's Trinity United Methodist or of Jacksonville's Simpson Memorial United Methodist came to Franklin Town. People looked forward to these summertime Thursday beach gatherings as though they were families gathering for the holidays. First they swam and fished, then they played ball, the churches pitted against each other, the teams cheered on by enthusiastic crowds.

When activities on the shore were over, the crowds retreated to the pavilion owned by Hayes Stewart, son-in-law of the old Union soldier Gabriel Means.[12] During the week, Stewart fished and prepared for the big weekend beach fish fry. He sold fish sandwiches for fifteen cents, and his wife made shrimp pilaf, or pilau (pronounced "purlo" locally), that they sold with the dinners. Stewart did not have a liquor license but served home brew for thirty cents a bottle. After the church crew left on Thursday evenings, Stewart's pavilion operated around the clock for the Fernandina and Old Town crowds, who partied all Saturday and Sunday night, then walked the ten or twelve miles back to town early Monday morning.

When Gabriel Means died in 1914, his funeral was held not at the church he built but in downtown Fernandina at the Trinity United Methodist Church to accommodate the large number of mourners. He is buried at Franklin Town Cemetery, a two-acre plot given by the Harrison family more than two centuries ago as a burial ground for plantation slaves and their families. The original Franklin Town church was bulldozed to make way for A1A in 1949 and a new sanctuary built in May of that year. In 1972 the new building was moved to its present location on American Beach, where it today serves as the church's fellowship hall.

For nearly a hundred years the Franklin Town community revolved around a few families, many of whom chose to live their entire lives on the southern end of Amelia Island east of highway A1A. Recent members of these families moved closer to the town of Fernandina or other nearby communities in Nassau and Duval Counties, where they bought their own land. In 1972, after a century of ownership, Franklin Town's remaining families sold the last of their beachfront and riverfront property to the Amelia Island Company, forerunner of Amelia Island Plantation, and moved one mile

Maintaining the grounds of the Franklin Town Cemetery is a labor of love for George Green, great-grandson of Civil War veteran Gabriel Means, laid to rest here in 1914. Former Franklin Town residents fought fiercely to prevent Plantation Point Joint Venture developer homes being built on grave sites. Courtesy Michael Phelts.

The home of Evelyn and William Thomas Jefferson, moved to American Beach from Franklin Town in 1972. Courtesy Michael Phelts.

These cousins, members of the fifth and sixth generations of the Means family on Amelia Island, are readying for a bicycle expedition around American Beach. The flag in the background is one of many prominently displayed in the community. Courtesy Michael Phelts.

north to American Beach. Here they live in the first full block of cottages along scenic, tree-lined Lewis Street, which leads straight to the ocean.

Means's great-grandchildren continue to maintain and nurture the Franklintown United Methodist Church, where services are held each Sunday and where various community groups meet weekly in the fellowship hall. The superintendent of the Sunday school, George Green, is a great-grandson of Means. Means's great-great-grandson, Philip Jefferson, a multitalented musician, plays at both African American United Methodist churches on Amelia Island. Today the church Means founded is a cornerstone of the American Beach community.

Franklin Town families take pride in a cultural and family heritage that can be documented through courthouse records and by an oral tradition. In talking with these families I was able to witness in practice chapter 1, verse 3 of Joel, in the Old Testament: "Tell ye your children of it, and let your children tell their children, and their children another generation." It was "another generation" that made it possible for me to record the way of life in Franklin Town, the forerunner of American Beach.

A. L. Lewis

Anything will give up its secrets if you love it enough.
GEORGE WASHINGTON CARVER

On March 29, 1865, two years after the Emancipation Proclamation, Abraham Lincoln Lewis was born free in Madison, Florida, and named by his parents, Julia Brown and Robert Lewis, for the Great Emancipator. The Civil War would officially end with General Robert E. Lee's surrender ten days later. As was true for both Lincoln and Lee, as for many men of vision and accomplishment, Lewis would eventually become the subject of larger-than-life legends. Throughout the state of Florida, from Jacksonville to Miami, schools, buildings, gateways, and streets would be named one day in his honor.

In 1876, at the age of eleven, Lewis and at least four brothers and sisters moved with his family from Madison to the east side of Jacksonville, where his father found work as a blacksmith. Young Lewis attended the Oakland Graded School until he found a job at the Dexter Hunter Lumber Mill on the corner of Florida Avenue and East Bay Street—the family needed even his meager water boy's wages. Over the twenty-two years young Lewis worked

East Jacksonville home of A. L. Lewis's father and stepmother, Robert and Charlotte Anderson Lewis, at 903 Jessie Street in 1994, demolished the next year. When Charlotte Lewis died in 1928 she was recognized as one of the oldest and most prosperous of the antebellum African Americans remaining in Jacksonville. Courtesy Michael Phelts.

at Dexter Hunter, he served as laborer and mechanic, and finally as fore-man, the highest-paid black man on the job.[1]

Marriage into the Kingsley-Sammis Dynasty

When he was nineteen, Lewis married Mary Sammis, the great-granddaugh-ter of the wealthy, eccentric slave trader, planter, writer, political activist, and landowner Zephaniah Kingsley and his Senegalese wife, Anna Jai. At forty-one, Kingsley brought the tall, beautiful, jet-black thirteen-year-old African to Florida. In his will, written in 1843, he left his family well pro-vided. It begins: "Whereas I am of sound mind and know what I am doing, and whereas I know perfectly well that it is against the laws and conven-tions of life to marry a colored person, and whereas this is my property and it is not any body's damn business what I do with it. . . ." He further writes: "And whereas I have an African wife, who is one of the finest women I have ever known and who has been true and faithful to me, . . . and whereas I know that what I am about to do is going to bring down upon me tre-mendous criticism, but I don't give a damn. Now therefore I give to my wife. . . ." He acknowledged his 1806 marriage in Senegal, explaining his wife's origins "in a foreign land where our marriage was celebrated and solemnized by her native African custom although never celebrated according to the forms of Christian usage: yet she has always been respected as my wife and as such I acknowledge her, nor do I think that her truth, honor, integrity, moral conduct or good sense will lose in comparison to anyone."[2] By the time she turned eighteen, Kingsley had freed her from slavery.[3] As the wife of the plantation owner and master, Anna Jai not only had many slaves of her own but helped her husband supervise other slaves, a task in which her familiarity with the Wolof language proved an asset. Anna Jai and Zephaniah Kingsley had four children—George, Martha, Mary, and John—who received good European educations. When his mulatto daughters were of marriageable age, Kingsley offered large sums of money to entice suitable white men to marry them.

Kingsley's plantations comprised more than 32,000 acres in north Florida, and his slave trading reached such proportions that he was able to build his own ships. Colonel John Sammis, a New Englander, came south to help build the boats, married the Kingsleys' youngest daughter, Mary Elizabeth, and settled in the Arlington area of Jacksonville. A man of wealth before his

"National troops marching through Second Street, New Fernandina, Florida," August 16, 1862, from a sketch by W. Crane. John S. Sammis and his family were then living on Amelia Island, where their granddaughter Mary Frances was born on February 3, 1865. Courtesy Florida State Archives.

Abraham Lincoln Lewis, ca. 1919. Lewis amassed a fortune in several enterprises and generously contributed to black colleges to aid in the education of his people. Courtesy Florida State Archives.

arranged marriage, Sammis greatly increased his holdings by marrying into the Kingsley family, acquiring a vast amount of land in Duval County; his name appeared on nearly every abstract of title to lands in the Arlington area.[4] He also owned several sawmills. The Sammises had four children who reached adulthood. Among them, Edward, a Duval County justice of the peace, would become the father of Mary, Abraham Lincoln Lewis's future wife, born in 1865 in Fernandina.[5] Although Zephaniah Kingsley died in 1843, his wife, his daughters, and their offspring remained free in Territorial Florida throughout the antebellum period. During the Civil War, Colonel John Sammis retreated with his family—as free mulattos—and his mother-in-law, Anna Jai Kingsley, to the safety of Fernandina when it was occupied by Union soldiers.

Sammis's political loyalties were somewhat fickle. A clerk once recorded this estimate of him: "Keeps his true feelings studiedly concealed, in Sept. 1861 at Nashville he taken an oath to Confederate Government voluntarily in November following taken oath of Allegiance to US as Louisville, Kentucky, came to Nashville taken another oath to Confederacy all for pecuniary purposes. Is extremely mercenary, has and would defraud Government out of duties on goods, unreliable in his dealings. Will resort to any means to make money. Thinks his money and property gives him influence."[6]

John Sammis had long shown a proclivity for amassing money. He became the executor of Zephaniah Kingsley's estate, representing Kingsley's widow and children, a position he held for forty years until his death in November 1883.[7] On Wednesday, October 29, 1884, at the Duval County Courthouse, A. L. Lewis and John Sammis's granddaughter, Mary Elizabeth Sammis, applied for their marriage license.[8] Like her husband-to-be, Mary Sammis was nineteen. Lewis brought to the marriage ambition and reliability; Mary Sammis brought a respected name and recognition. Many people either did not know of or would not acknowledge her direct descent from Zephaniah and Anna Kingsley, but something about Mary Lewis set her apart from most of her friends and neighbors.

Prosperity and Laundry on Sugar Hill

At age twenty-three, in 1888, Lewis became partner in a black-owned shoe store. In 1891, Mary Lewis was elected chair of the first Deaconess Board in Bethel Baptist Institutional Church, a position she held for at least twenty years and perhaps until she died. Meanwhile, A. L. Lewis and six other forward-looking black men founded the Afro-American Industrial and Benefit Association in 1901, forerunner of the Afro-American Life Insurance Company. The idea for a burial insurance company came from Milton Waldron, the influential pastor of Jacksonville's Bethel Baptist Institutional Church from 1892 until 1907. At the time, for ten cents a week, members of the church's burial society could receive a burial benefit of $30. Waldron suggested that the society be moved out of the church and made nondenominational so that any citizen might take part; he recommended E. J. Gregg, pastor of Mt. Zion AME Church, as the new company's president.[9]

By 1914, the Lewises and their son, James Henry, had moved from the east side of town to 504 West Eighth Street directly across the park from Springfield, exclusive, whites-only suburb. Lewis had a grand home constructed for his family at the entrance of an affluent Springfield Heights neighborhood called Sugar Hill. Joseph H. Blodgett built the Lewis home as well as an ornate home for his family. Blodgett and Lewis were acknowledged as the first black millionaires in Florida. Even after their move to this magnificent home, Mary Lewis continued to do the laundry of a long-time customer. Each Monday morning, the chauffeur of a Jacksonville bank executive would drop off the banker's shirts for laundering.

Afro-American Life Insurance Company

REV. J. MILTON WALDON, D.D.
(Deceased)

REV. E. J. GREGG, D.D.
(Deceased)

" "T o P" "

E. W. LATSON
(Deceased)

DR. A. L. LEWIS
Chairman of Board of Directors

A. W. PRICE
(Deceased)

DECEASED - 1947

JAMES FRANKLIN VALENTINE
(Deceased)

DR. ARTHUR WALLS SMITH
Practicing Physician

At the request of J. Milton Waldron, these seven men came together on January 15, 1901, in Bethel Baptist Institutional Church in Jacksonville to found the Afro-American Industrial and Benefit Association. Each pledged a hundred dollars to start the corporation. The state of Florida granted a charter on March 1, 1901, and the Reverend E. J. Gregg was elected president. From top left: Rev. J. Milton Waldron, Rev. E. J. Gregg, E. W. Latson, A. L. Lewis, A. W. Price, James Franklin Valentine, and Dr. Arthur Walls Smith. Courtesy Saramae Stewart Richardson.

In 1919, Lewis became president and board chair of the Afro-American Life Insurance Company, whose capital, surplus, and assets increased steadily under his administration. Lewis received a salary of $1,000 a month by 1926, while the other top Afro executives took home $500 monthly, department heads $225, and agents $150 plus commission.[10] At the time, auto mechanics were earning $48 a month, section foremen $5 a day; brick masons $1.25 an hour, and loggers doing roadwork $4.50 a day.

In the early 1920s, Lewis began investing in real estate, taking advantage of a number of resourceful contacts who were well connected with Nassau County landowners. Eartha Mary Magdalene White, the first female employee of the Afro in its founding year, was well known and respected by business and civic leaders and proved an invaluable broker for Lewis in many of his land negotiations. White had long since proved her loyalty to the company; when much of Jacksonville was destroyed by fire on May 3, 1901, she had moved all Afro's records to Lewis's home.[11]

Combined with her loyalty and integrity, her family history and connections made her the perfect contact for Lewis's real estate interests. A descendant of pioneer slave and plantation families on Amelia Island, White was related to the Stockton, Drummond, Means, Green, and Harrison families. Her biological father was Guy Stockton, from a prominent white family. Eartha's mother, Clara English White, was born on the Harrison plantation on July 4, 1845. As a child, Clara watched as her mother, Eartha's grandmother, Jane Drummond English, was sold away from her children and husband at a slave auction in Jacksonville. Later, Mary Magdalene Cooper Harrison, wife of the plantation owner, Robert Harrison, presented Clara to her nephew, Colonel Charles Cooper, as a birthday gift.[12] Clara continued to work for Cooper after emancipation. Clara also was employed in 1886 by the Rollins family, new owners of Kingsley's plantation, where she and her daughter, Eartha White, lived. Though Kingsley was long dead and his mulatto family scattered, many former slave families continued to homestead in the tabby slave quarters on the plantation.

Eartha White knew Kingsley's and Sammis's descendants quite well. As a young woman, she was wooed by Albert Sammis Jr., the grandson of Colonel John Sammis. Neither of them married, and, upon Albert Jr.'s death in 1943, his friend Eartha White became executor of his will. He also left her land that his grandfather had owned. With her influential contacts and resources, Eartha White easily assisted A. L. Lewis to meet the right people.

Eartha White and her mother, Clara English White, ca. 1910. Courtesy Florida State Archives.

During the winter of 1923, at the age of fifty-eight, Mary Lewis became ill. Although a nurse was brought in to stay with her around the clock, she died within the week of a cerebral hemorrhage. (The nurse, Annie Reed, later married the Lewises' only child, James Henry.)[13] Mary Lewis was first buried in the Duval Cemetery. Some years later, A. L. Lewis began plans for a family mausoleum, and Mary Lewis was reinterred there upon its completion in 1939. Their great-granddaughters remember family trips to the cemetery every Sunday after church during beach off-season and watching their great-grandfather sit on a marble bench inside the mausoleum to meditate for long periods of time.

Nearly two years after Mary Lewis's death, Lewis married Elzona Burney, the organist for Mt. Olive AME Church, where Lewis served as superintendent of the Sunday school for fifty-seven years.

In 1928, at the age of sixty-three, Lewis organized and became president of the Fifty-Fifty Bottling Company, the first company of its kind owned and controlled by blacks. Co-owners and officers of this company were his son, James Henry Lewis, Louis D. Ervin, and William H. Lee. The bottling company of these Afro executives furnished all bottled drinks of soda water, retail and resale, with three branches in the state of Florida.[14]

During the Depression, Afro-American Life Insurance Company executives and employees continued to fare well, even with salary cuts. Lewis's salary as president decreased to $666 a month. His dividends from company stocks, which soared into the thousands, now greatly exceeded his $7,992 annual salary.[15] In September 1930 Lewis traveled to Detroit with

Interred in the Lewis family mausoleum at Memorial Cemetery are A. L. Lewis (d. 1947); his first wife, Mary Sammis (d. 1923); their son, James Henry Lewis (d. 1975); their grandson, James Leonard Lewis (d. 1954); A. L. Lewis's sister Eliza Lewis Dixon (d. 1959); and Lewis's widow, Elzona Lewis Nobileo (d. 1966). Courtesy Michael Phelts.

Abraham Lincoln Lewis, last surviving founder of the Afro-American Life Insurance Company, and his wife, Mary Sammis Lewis. Date unknown. Courtesy Eartha White Collection, University of North Florida Library, Jacksonville.

two staff members, Prof. A. St. George Richardson and B. C. Daughtry, to purchase a new Lincoln Town Sedan. He paid $3,500 for this chauffeur-driven car in just twelve months.[16] Throughout the Depression the company invested in real estate, taking advantage of foreclosures—in 1935 came the purchase by the company's Pension Bureau of what would one day be American Beach.

As the country went to war in 1941, salaries at the Afro had regained their pre-Depression levels. Then in its fortieth anniversary year, the Afro patted itself on the back in a company history: "The highest salaried men and women of our race in our state are found on the semi-monthly payroll of the Afro-American Life Insurance Company, a company who for forty years

A. L. Lewis with his son, grandchildren, and nephews. Bottom row, left to right: Lewis's great-granddaughters Bertha Johnnetta and Marvyne Elizabeth Betsch, grand nephew Fred Dixon Jr., and granddaughter Mary Francis Lewis Betsch. Middle row, left to right: nephew Fred Dixon Sr., A. L. and Elzona Burney Lewis, great-grandson James L. Lewis, daughter-in-law Annie Reed Lewis. Top row, left to right: niece Florence Dixon, grandson-in-law John T. Betsch, granddaughter-in-law Nellie Lewis, James Henry Lewis. Courtesy Marvyne Betsch.

has never missed a payday or for any cause delayed salary payment."[17] The twenty-eight years of Lewis's administrative reign were the most productive the company had ever seen. Company stock rose from $1 to $100 a share.

LOCAL AND NATIONAL RECOGNITION

In 1947, Lewis owned more property and paid more property taxes than any black person in the state of Florida.[18] As far back as 1891, he had begun exploring a grant for some land that had belonged to Mary Lewis's great-grandfather, Zephaniah Kingsley. It was eventually deeded to him for the development of the thirty-six-acre Lincoln Golf and Country Club, an exclusive recreational facility that opened in 1929 just of U.S. 1. The broad stream on the golf course, known as the six-mile stream, was a favorite community fishing spot where large catfish and bream were considered prize catches. The public continued to have free access to fishing. Guests at the club could choose from a range of amenities: a nine-hole golf course, dining room, clubhouse, swimming pool, shooting range, two clay tennis courts, picnic facilities, and a recreational playground for children.[19]

Far more than an entrepreneur, Lewis has been credited as the leading force behind several historic building projects still standing in Jacksonville, including Mt. Olive AME (he chaired the church's building committee when construction began in 1921), the five-story, reinforced-concrete and brick Masonic Temple, and the Lewis family mausoleum. He also gave generously and often to educational institutions, orphanages, churches, and charities without regard to race. A natural leader with a good mind for finance,

Installation dinner for officers and directors of the Lincoln Golf and Country Club at the annual Christmas party, 1950. Left to right: Charles "Logger" Sheppard, George Harris, Melvin Ward, John Henry "Jack" Jackson, Ernest "Mint" Jones, Clarence "Spider" Jefferson, Curtis Taylor, Joseph Crawford, Joseph Gardner, James Burris, Oscar Fletcher, and William Shellman. Courtesy Curtis Taylor.

Lewis worked with Booker T. Washington to establish the National Negro Business League.

After Lewis's death in 1947, the Lincoln Golf and Country Club was given to Lewis's grandson, James Leonard. In 1954 Lewis's great-grandson, Little James, inherited the golf club when his father died suddenly. Little James sold the property to a white-owned firm, Carver Construction Company, in the early 1960s. Since then it has become a middle-class black housing development, the Lincoln Estates and Carver Manor subdivisions, just off highway U.S. 1 and Richardson Road. Golfers and country club owners felt their saddest hours in the closing days of the Lincoln Golf and Country Club. While removing celebrity pictures from the clubhouse walls, Curtis Taylor's tears fell like summer rain. Elwood "Homie" Banks, who played eighteen holes in the 1930s and 1940s for 25 cents laments, "There is no trace of where the golf course used to be."[20]

CHAPTER 4

A Beach Named American

These are my people, I have built for them / A castle in the cloister of my heart
FENTON JOHNSON

The Afro-American Industrial and Benefit Association . . . the Afro-American Life Insurance Company . . . Lincoln Golf and Country Club . . . American Beach—when A. L. Lewis had a hand in naming something, his fondness for the grand and the historic, for *honoring* and paying homage, was apparent. When it came to naming the buildings and streets of American Beach, bought by Afro-American Life Insurance Pension Bureau funds, only one—Ocean Street—would not carry a name tied directly to Lewis by family or history.

BUYING A BEACH

In the 1920s and early 1930s, the Afro-American Insurance Company frequently sponsored beach outings on Amelia Island in Franklin Town, where beachgoers drove from the highway to the beach along a dirt trail so narrow that they could only leave in reverse order, each car backing in turn out to the road.[1] Based on the popularity of these outings, Lewis sought ocean-front land for a resort community for his company and their families. When

Curtis Taylor leased and managed the Lincoln Golf and Country Club from 1947 to 1959. Left to right: waitress Lucille Puzie, head cook Virginia Brown, and Taylor, in 1948. Courtesy Curtis Taylor.

the available property in Franklin Town proved too small for what he had in mind, his friend, Hayes Stewart of Franklin Town, put Lewis in touch with Lasserre Realty for the purchase of property north of Franklin Town.

Once they had settled on a price, the realtor doubted whether Lewis had the means to pay for the property. Lewis is alleged to have told him, "I've been saving money all my life."[2] That year, 1935, the Afro boasted of "35 years of success" with paid-up capital stock of $200,000.

Afro's Pension Bureau, the buyer of record, actually purchased the American Beach property in three parcels over eleven years. The first 33-acre parcel was part of the Suhrer Tract, named for the astute tax collector who bought it in 1875. Thick with live oak, palm, pine, bay, magnolia, and walnut trees, its eighty-six acres were bounded by the Atlantic Ocean to the east and the Amelia River to the west, rich with game, fish, and shellfish. In a deal—or a steal—that looks slightly questionable in hindsight, the tax collector, Ferdinand Charles Suhrer Jr., paid $6.71 for the property on the auction block because its owner was delinquent in paying taxes on it.[3] On the other hand, Suhrer, a native of the Grand Duchy of Baden in Germany, had served as an officer of the Union Army during the Civil War and held many offices of public trust in federal, state, and municipal government. Then again, while serving as president of the City Council of Fernandina, Suhrer was killed at his home on February 8, 1884, reportedly in a dispute with a boarder, Thomas Jefferson Eppes, Jr., son of Judge T. J. Eppes of Monticello, Florida, and a great-great-grandson of Thomas Jefferson.[4]

At the turn of the twentieth century, Suhrer's widow Eva Rosa Suhrer sold the whole tract to Alfred Lucas for $800, about a 1,200% profit on Suhrer's original purchase price.[5] Property titles of the Suhrer Tract changed hands again after Lucas's death in 1924. For the next ten years, one investor after another held title to these undeveloped shores.

On January 31, 1935, the Pension Bureau bought the first of the three parcels for $2,000 from the estate of Richard Delafield—thirty-three acres, with a thousand feet fronting on the ocean.[6] The parcel's boundaries can be traced today in American Beach: from Mary Street on the west to Lewis Street on the south, the ocean on the east, and Julia Street on the north. Develop-

Major Ferdinand C. Suhrer Jr., ca. 1865. At one time owner of the American Beach tract, Suhrer managed the Mansion House, a popular hotel for railroad workers and tourists. He was murdered on the steps of the hotel by T. J. Eppes, a conductor on the Florida Transit and Peninsular Railroad. Courtesy Mr. and Mrs. Clarence Lohman; Florida State Archives.

Eva Rosa Plotts Suhrer, ca. 1865. The widow of Ferdinand Suhrer Jr., Eva Suhrer sold eighty-six acres of coastal property in 1902, a portion of the land that would become American Beach. Courtesy Mr. and Mrs. Clarence Lohman; Florida State Archives.

ment began immediately, with streets being cut and lots surveyed and sold. The Afro Pavilion and homes went up.

The Afro bought the adjoining second parcel, a hundred acres, from Olin and Cornelia Watts in 1937.[7] Based on the number of documents required for this transaction, the Pension Bureau apparently first needed a white agent to buy the property and then sell it to the Afro; Olin Watts, a white lawyer whose firm represented Lewis and the Afro for many years, served that purpose. Until then, the land had been passed and sold down the line to members of the Harrison family right along with the slaves on their plantation. When a Harrison daughter, son, or relative married, land titles were transferred and slaves reassigned to ensure the new family wouldn't lack the proper Harrison amenities and services. The tract today begins at AIA, the First Coast Highway, on the west, and runs between Burney Road and Lewis Street to Ocean Boulevard on the east.

The third parcel of land, eighty-three acres with a fifteen-hundred-foot shoreline, was granted to the Pension Bureau of the Afro by the U.S. government in 1946 during the presidency of Harry S Truman.[8] American Beach was now a community of 216 contiguous acres with a half-mile ocean front.

The first streets built in American Beach were named after four of the Afro's seven founders.[9]

The very first—the main thoroughfare and the only street allowing vehicular beach access—was Lewis Street, named for the Afro chairman of the board. All but two of the other streets intersect with Lewis. Both Julia Street and Burney Road run east-west parallel to Lewis Street.

Gregg, the first street parallel to the ocean, honors the Reverend Elias J. Gregg, pastor of the Mt. Zion AME Church and the first president of the Afro-American Industrial and Benefit Association when it was chartered in 1901. Inland from Gregg lies Ocean Boulevard, a road that ran through dunes and offered a commanding view of the Atlantic.

The third street from the ocean, and that with the highest elevation, was named for J. Milton Waldron, the influential pastor of Jacksonville's Bethel Baptist Institutional Church from 1892 until 1907, upon whose idea the Afro was built. To Waldron Street's west lies Price, named for the Reverend Alfred W. Price, the third president of the Afro-American Life Insurance Company. As president, Price established a savings bank. During the 1870s and early 1880s, Price, a retail grocer, had also served as a deputy sheriff, later as a Duval County constable. His grandson, Albert W. Price III, and Zora Neale Hurston were married in the Nassau County Courthouse in 1939.

As beach development progressed, new streets were given the names of Lewis's immediate family members, high-ranking company executives, and patriots. James Street honored James H. Lewis, the only surviving child of Mary and A. L. Lewis; having served as the Afro's auditor and vice-president, he succeeded his father as president a year after the founding of American Beach.

The Afro's first full-time agent in 1901, Louis Dargan Ervin, gave his name to Ervin Street. A skilled masonry contractor, Ervin stayed with the company for sixty-three years, moving up the corporate ladder to inspector, auditor, superintendent, manager, director, cashier, and finally vice-president. Lee Street was named for the Honorable William H. Lee, secretary, vice president, and board member of the Afro and a brigadier general commanding the Florida Brigade of the Uniform Rank, Knights of Pythias (a secret benevolent and fraternal order), widely respected for his oratory ability. He had previously been a public school teacher and post office clerk in his native Atlanta, Georgia.

Leonard Street was named for James Leonard Lewis, grandson of the president and a graduate of Morehouse College and New York University Law School before he signed on with the Afro. Mary Street honored Mary Lewis, A. L. Lewis's first wife, and Julia Street, the second east-west street leading to the ocean, honored his mother, Julia Brown Lewis. Prior to the 1970s, Julia Street was no more than a trail that went as far west as Gus Logan's Barbecue Stand and Rooming House at the corner of Mary Street, where there was always a lot of action. In the mid-1970s, the west end of Julia Street became the southern end of the Amelia Island Parkway.

I. H. Burney II, for whom Burney Road was named, was president of the Afro-American Life Insurance Company from 1967 to 1975 and the only one since A. L. Lewis's presidency who was not Lewis's blood relative or son-in-law. This east-west road was the last road developed on American Beach.

Additional streets named in the 1940s but never developed included (Booker T.) Washington, (George Washington) Carver, (Abraham) Lincoln, and (William) McKinley—the president was assassinated the year the Afro was founded. Also unbuilt was Stewart Street, named to honor the Afro's secretary Ralph Stewart Sr., a graduate of Tuskegee Institute in Alabama and president of the Tuskegee Alumni Association. Stewart vigorously recruited the school's alumni and staff to purchase vacation property on American Beach. (His sons, Ralph Jr. and Dennis, were graduates of Tuskegee during the early 1940s when the streets were named; Ralph Jr. served as an assistant in the laboratory of Dr. George Washington Carver.)[10]

CHAPTER 5

Early Homes

This is our home and this is our country. Beneath its soil lie the bones of our fathers; for it some of them fought, bled, and died. Here we were born and here we will stay.

PAUL ROBESON

Less than seven months after the purchase of the first tract of land for American Beach, contractor Willie S. Rivers completed work on the community's first oceanfront house.[1]

Construction of private homes on the oceanfront began as soon after purchase of the first tract of land as sites could be cleared. Plumbing for the early homes was contracted to Rudolph G. Lohman, of German descent, whose wife's parents, Ferdinand and Eva Rosa Suhrer, had once owned the tract of land that became American Beach.[2] Rudolph Lohman Jr. was sixteen years old when he worked with his father on American Beach for ten cents an hour. At the end of the week, Rudy handed his earnings over to his parents to help toward his board and keep.

The first home on American Beach, finished by Willie Rivers on August 24, 1935, on lot 12, block 2, belonged to A. L. Lewis.

Early American Beach homes. On the far left is the home of Carey Freeman, built in 1937 (Freeman was Lewis's dentist). The center home was completed in 1935 for A. L. Lewis. After the home on the right was completed, it became A. L. Lewis's, and the first-built home went to his son, James. The car in the driveway is Lewis's 1930 chauffeur-driven Lincoln. Courtesy Ernestine Latson Smith.

Known throughout the island for his craftsmanship, Rivers also built the pavilion and the cabins that the Afro reserved for their executives, employees, and celebrated guests. The pavilion, constructed for public use, offered no lodging but included a restaurant and bath house.

After finishing the pavilion and the cabins, Rivers built another home on lot 13 for A. L. Lewis in 1938. Lewis then sold the first home to his son. Lewis and his second wife, Elzona, moved into the stately new home, solidly constructed, which has now stood through many storms and major hurricanes, even though Hurricane Dora in 1964 rearranged its crisscross stairs. Since 1960, the family of N. E. and Johnnie Fluker, from Waycross, Georgia, has owned A. L. Lewis's oceanfront home. The Flukers' son, Carlton, and other family members have restored this wooden structure to its architectural splendor.

The homes of Louis Dargan Ervin and Ralph Stewart are the only houses built in the first decade of the beach that are still owned by their descendants. These two homes have never been sold but have been passed down to the children and grandchildren of the original owners.

Louis Dargan Ervin was the first agent for the Afro and, at the time of the founding of American Beach, the company's general manager.[3] His only daughter, Mabel, married Ernest Latson, the son of an Afro founder, E. W. Latson. Ernestine Latson Smith, granddaughter of both Ervin and Latson, and her husband, Samuel, now occupy the home, a year-round retreat for their five daughters and their families. Ernestine's most poignant memories are the sounds of pebbles thrown against her window at 5:30 in the mornings as the sun rose from the ocean. Her childhood friend from Atlanta, Louis Reese (now a physician there), threw the pebbles to awaken her for their first swim of the day. In the evening breezes, the Reese and Latson families enjoyed playing cards. Reese and his mother were card sharks, beating Ernestine and her mother each time they played, until the day Ernestine's brother looked in Louis's hand and saw straight across into Mrs. Reese's hand from the reflection of the sunglasses she always wore while playing cards.[4]

For years the home of Ralph and Marie Stewart stood as the lone cottage on the highest elevated street on American Beach, where lots run the depth

The restored former home of A. L. Lewis, since 1960 the home of the N. C. Fluker family. Many of the original furnishings have been retained. Courtesy Michael Phelts.

Louis Ervin built the second home on American Beach. His signature, along with that of A. L. Lewis, is on transactions of early American Beach documents. Ervin started with the Afro in 1901 and advanced from agent to first vice president and cashier, giving the company sixty-three years of dedicated service. Courtesy Michael Phelts.

of the entire street from front to back. The shingle structure has well withstood the ravages of nature for more than fifty years. In the 1950s it was designated an official party house for picnics sponsored by the Afro. The tradition continues today, with Stewart's grandchildren and great-grandchildren spending many happy hours in a place they dearly love.

Other lasting contributions by the Stewarts to the community are the history of the Afro written by Ralph and the history of St. Philips Episcopal Church by Marie.

In 1937, a home was built on American Beach for Carey Verdell Freeman, born August 19, 1884, on Amelia Island and the president of the Negro Business League.[5]

After graduating from Howard University in Washington, D.C., Freeman had established a successful dental practice in Jacksonville. He and his wife, Arabell Cambridge, were among the first to invest in property on American Beach. Their two-story oceanfront home resembled the insides of a ship, with portholes for windows, wooden racks for beds, and a small dinghy stored under the steep, narrow stairwell. In the early days, the Freemans swung on a rope from the berths to the lower deck. On the mess deck a huge mahogany table with carvings of many sea creatures remains a conversation piece today. Ernestine Latson Smith, who lived next door to the Freemans, reminisced about the many galas her parents and family members enjoyed at the unique beach home.

After Carey Freeman's death and with his widow's health failing, the home was sold to their friend Elizabeth Cobb of Tuskegee, Alabama. For years Cobb spent every summer there, bringing an entourage of family and friends, as well as a nanny for her nieces and nephews. When the journeys to American Beach taxed her health, Cobb sold the home in 1959 to her protégée, Emma Morgan, and her husband, Frank. The Morgans' family and guests continue to enjoy many of the original furnishings, antiques, and nautical gems of the house's former owners.

Miss Martha's Hideaway

And when I cried out with mother's grief, none but Jesus heard—
and ain't I a woman?
SOJOURNER TRUTH

While company executives were selecting home sites with ocean views, Martha Hippard, a widow, was building a home in an area of American Beach that remains secluded to this day. On an acre deep in the woods, Hippard's house was constructed of hand-hewn coquina blocks and hand-molded bricks. To make these blocks, Frank Johnson, a master of trades, hauled truckloads of crushed shell from the American Beach coquina beds to Miss Martha's building site. Here he mixed two parts coquina with one part cement and made two blocks at a time, pouring the mixture into two 16 x 8 x 8 molds. After shaping, the blocks were removed from the molds and sundried in the yard. Since the other homes sat on lots that measured fifty by a hundred feet, hers stood out, one of the grandest structures on the beach. Miss Martha furnished this palatial hideaway with beautiful pieces crafted by her father, Brooks Thompson, widely known for his fine handiwork.

Miss Martha had much influence in Fernandina, where at 20 North Third Street she owned and operated the Plum Garden, a restaurant, lounge, and

Hanna Mitchell (left)
and Miss Martha
Hippard vacationing in
Havana, late 1940s.
During her heyday Miss
Martha carried money
to the bank in cigar
boxes. Courtesy Cecil
Williams.

rooftop bar beautifully decorated with live palm trees and tropical plants.
But her notoriety stemmed from the small coquina structure she had built
behind her home, to which prominent Georgians and Floridians came bear-
ing boxes of money to gamble at her high-stakes tables. She was one of the
most powerful people in the area, her word as good as a written contract.
Miss Martha and her first husband, Lemuel Hippard, also owned a bakery
and grocery store. People remember passing Miss Martha along the sidewalk going into the bank with her own money in a cigar box. She would
tip her head, say "Howdy do?" and keep on walking.

Often when the Plum Gardens closed in the wee hours of the morning,
Rufus Johnson, Miss Martha's chauffeur, drove her select party to the pri-

Rufus Johnson, the only boy in Peck High School's class of 1937, danced a caper to class from these steps in front of the school every morning. Courtesy Rufus Johnson.

vacy of her American Beach property, where the gambling might continue for twelve hours or more. A schoolmate and friend of the Hippards' only child, Sarah Elizabeth, Johnson had chauffeured Miss Martha since he was a teenager (she wanted to hire someone who didn't drink) and had known her family all his life. His grandfather and Miss Martha's father built the home for Johnson's mother when she married. Johnson remembered Lemuel Hippard for sponsoring boat excursions from Fernandina to Savannah and for carrying a suitcase filled with money.

Rufus Johnson recalled one Friday when he went to the Plum Gardens straight from school. It was early in the evening of May 22, 1936. Business was rather slow due to a drizzling rain, and a group decided to have Johnson drive them over to Jacksonville—Miss Martha's second husband, Griffin Simmons, her fifteen-year-old daughter, Sarah, her close friend Gwen Benton, and a boy about ten years old whom they called Dummy (because he couldn't talk). Johnson rushed home to change into city clothes and returned to Plum Gardens to find that the car had left without him, with Miss Martha's husband driving. About 8:30 that night Miss Martha answered the telephone, screamed, "Oh, my God!" and flung the wall phone from her hand. There had been an accident in the 17000 block of North Main Street, near the Ole Plantation Lounge on the outskirts of Jacksonville. The roads were slippery. The car was going too fast to make the curve; the speedometer locked on eight-five. All in the car were killed instantly: Miss Martha's only child, her husband, her best friend, and the little boy.[1]

Rudolph Williams, who eventually replaced Rufus Johnson as Miss Martha's chauffeur, was, like his predecessor, old enough to drive but not old enough to drink. An American Beach resident, Williams tells of the times when, as a teenager, he drove Miss Martha on junkets out of town. Upon arrival, she would check him into a rooming house, then drive her black, custom, deluxe Ford to gambling hideaways so private even her chauffeur could not know of them. When Williams, at the age of nineteen, and his

Miss Martha's dad, Brooks Thompson, handcrafted these child-size furnishings for his granddaughter Sarah Hippard. After Sarah was killed in an auto accident in 1936, her mother gave these pieces to the little girl next door, Gwendolyn Miller. Miller, Nassau County tax collector since 1976, gave these treasures to her own granddaughter for Christmas in 1996. Courtesy Gwendolyn Miller.

bride, Terethal Christopher, bought their first home, Miss Martha co-signed the mortgage.[2]

Not everyone recalls Miss Martha's activities in the same way. Her godsister, Cecil Williams, told me that what outsiders called the gambling house on American Beach was in fact an entertainment house, a setting for dances and club parties for civic and fraternal organizations—even churches—and for big family dinner parties. Williams acknowledged that a lot of merriment took place on American Beach when Miss Martha entertained. As to the splendor of the grand coquina house and its furnishings, Williams said that there was no comparison between the beach house and Miss Martha's house in downtown Fernandina. Miss Martha had always been accustomed to fine living, and the house in Fernandina was even more lavish than the one on the beach.[3]

Brooks Thompson built his daughter a grand house in Fernandina. He also carved furnishings such as beds, tables, sofas, and hearths for the home. With a pocketknife he whittled intricate designs on the pieces, many of which are still in service. Thompson had died by the time his only child built on the beach. Miss Martha selected many of her father's hand carvings to furnish the new home.

In 1953, Miss Martha lost her grand American Beach home and all its furnishings to her eccentric friend, Lottie Orleana Harris, of nearby St. Marys, Georgia, to pay off gambling debts.

Miss Lottie was principal and teacher of the Camden County Training High School in St. Marys and had also been a Jeanes supervisor in the national program named for and funded by the Anna T. Jeanes Foundation. As a Jeanes supervisor, Miss Lottie traveled throughout the state teaching domestic science to families in rural areas. Miss Martha's hideaway became Miss Lottie's American Beach vacation home.[4]

As Miss Lottie neared her life's end in 1959, she offered to sell the home to Elmo and Annette Myers, who had honeymooned there as her guests three years earlier. Elmo Myers was the son of a well-established St. Marys family, Annette Myers an Amelia Island native. Miss Lottie wanted to ensure that her home would continue to have caring owners. The eager young couple bought it immediately. Within a year, both Miss Martha and her friend Miss Lottie had died.

The Myers converted Miss Martha's infamous coquina party house into a two-car garage but maintained the main house in its original splendor in-

Miss Martha's Hideaway, a grand home, pales next to her downtown Fernandina home, which her father, Brooks Thompson, built. The smaller building in the left background was originally a party house, converted by the present owners into a garage. Courtesy Michael Phelts.

side and out. The lacquered hardwood floors in every room have been well kept up and so have the walls, the columns, and all parts of the house.

Miss Martha found a master craftsman, Frank Xavier Mayer, who came from the village of Sonthofen in Germany, to do the carpentry for her American Beach hideaway. Mayer had moved with his bride from Jacksonville during the Fernandina Beach building boom of 1936. His skills earned a respectable name for him throughout the remainder of his life.

Miss Martha's landscaping plan has been maintained through the years. The giant spider lilies that she planted continue to bloom, as do the formosa azaleas planted in the eastward dunes surrounding her fortress. The old liquor bottles flung in these dunes keep the silence of so many stories!

I first heard tales about the legendary Miss Martha Hippard in 1966, the year I bought my first car, a 1966 Mustang, and partied on the beach until I was ready to come home. I was in a party that ended up at Miss Martha's that summer, at a gathering hosted by Marie and Jim Williams, caretakers for the Myerses, who lived in Guyana. The Williamses made periodic visits to check on the house, "Guyana," from their home in St. Marys and opened the hideaway to revelry when they house-sat on weekends, a tradition the house seemed to invite.

On a wintry January morning thirty years later, the Myerses awoke to the sound of bulldozers and backhoes felling trees in the centuries-old woods, making way for expansion at Summer Beach, their most immediate neighbors. The well-worn trail that ran across the highway and off the road, winding through the woods to the fine coquina structure, was bulldozed under. Now, a paved road leads to Miss Martha's stately dwelling. Lately, Annette Myers has been considering converting the home into a bed-and-breakfast inn, reviving the splendor of Miss Martha's era.

Ocean-Vu-Inn

My search for knowledge of things took me into many
strange places and adventures.
ZORA NEALE HURSTON

To build the first privately owned public lodging facility on American Beach, Ralph and Ada Lee, longtime friends of A. L. Lewis, had to challenge a clause in their deed that forbade the erection of any building for the private or public sale of intoxicating liquors or for the use or maintenance of a public nuisance.[1]

LEE'S OCEAN-VU-INN

In 1945, the Lees already had two homes on the beach. They rented out their first home to a few select people but realized that thousands of beach-goers—people who traveled to American Beach from as far away as Washington, D.C.—had no means or personal connections for overnight accommodations.[2] The couple decided to build a dining and lodging facility, which they would open to the public, and to advertise the sale of beer and wine along with other amenities.

At the time, the Lees were well established in northeast Florida business, social, and civic circles. They owned property in Jacksonville and the city of Fernandina as well as in American Beach; in fact, some people thought they owned the beach. Theirs was an industrious family with each member contributing to the well-being and development of the family business. The Lees' daughters, Gertrude Styles and Gwendolyn Bell, had helped build both the family beach cottages.

But with Lee's Ocean-Vu-Inn, a twenty-one-suite facility with a dining and ballroom, Gwen, the younger daughter, had had quite enough. Carrying hammers, nails, buckets, and boards, as well as providing services to an inn filled with guests was not her idea of beach living. She married at the age of seventeen.

Along with the other Lees and the A. L. Lewises, Gwen's life was entwined with that of the prominent educator Mary McLeod Bethune, an old family friend. Bethune had been an agent for the Afro in its early years, before she founded Bethune-Cookman College, and was a member of the company's board of directors in the 1940s. She had long counted on the Lees for help in organizing her network of groups to create nationwide coalitions. Al-

Over the objection of A. L. Lewis, Lee's Ocean-Vu-Inn opened in 1945 with a restaurant, a ballroom, and twenty-one guest rooms. Courtesy Selma Richardson.

The Lee family, July 1949. Standing from left: Ada Lee, Ralph Lee (holding granddaughter Bennye Langley), Gertrude Styles, Gwen Langley, and William Langley Sr. William Jr. is standing front center. Courtesy Gwen L. Bell.

though she had little time for relaxation, Bethune occasionally stayed with Ralph and Ada Lee at the Ocean-Vu-Inn, a circumstance that prompted her own interest in acquiring beach property for blacks in Daytona Beach. Along with other black leaders in Daytona, she established Bethune Beach in Volusia County in 1940. Gwen Lee Langley (now Bell), by then a student at Daytona's Bethune-Cookman College, posed on the rooftop of the beautiful Welricha Motel in a national advertising campaign for Bethune Beach—much more in line with her idea of what life at the beach should be.[3]

Duck's Ocean-Vu-Inn

In 1952, the Lees sold their inn to Alonzo and Pauline Davis. Alonzo Davis came to the island as a successful entrepreneur of the Duck Inn in downtown Jacksonville; that same year, he changed the name of his American Beach enterprise to Duck's Ocean-Vu-Inn.

Duck's featured seafood, along with the barbecue for which Davis was famous, and the sounds of jazz filled the inn's public rooms. Pictures of Cab Calloway, Ethel Waters, and Louise Beavers became part of the decor; such photos attracted jazz lovers and let others know they were in the wrong place as soon as the door swung open. Duck's clientele enjoyed a more relaxed atmosphere than could be found in the vigorous crowds at other establishments on the oceanfront.

On Mondays and Tuesdays, resort workers from the nearby Golden Isles in Georgia kept Duck's full, taking their days off after busy weekends, along with such weekend workers as morticians and bolita people. Bolita was played the same way as the Florida lottery operates in the 1990s except that it was illegal. People who played bolita placed their bets on numbers with a bolita person. When their numbers came in, they came to the beach, spending lavishly.

The Ocean-Vu-Inn is the lone building in the background in this late 1940s photo. The cars are parked on the shoulders of Lewis Street, then a dirt road. (The oyster shell paving was not laid until the 1950s.) In the foreground is a refreshment stand. Courtesy Ernestine Smith.

A typical 1940s beach crowd at the entrance ramp to the ocean. Courtesy Ernestine Smith.

The guest books kept for twenty years at Duck's show the same visitors coming year after year—from throughout Florida and from all over the state of Alabama, as if they were just crossing the county line; from San Francisco, Colorado Springs, Chicago, St. Louis, and Detroit; from Tennessee, Texas, and Ohio; and from all along the East Coast, from Massachusetts and Connecticut to Georgia.

And no wonder. Duck's Ocean-Vu-Inn was renowned for its pleasing food, music, and ambiance. The menu boasted a delectable range of dishes, including thick and tender steaks, fried chicken, pork chops, seafood, and homemade french fries. The most popular dinners were fried chicken and crab patties—seafood and chicken were bought fresh, seasoned, and then fried. Frequent trips to the docks at the foot of Centre Street in downtown Fernandina were part of the routine. There, in the mid-1950s, just-picked crabmeat sold for fifty cents a pound and shrimp for twenty-five cents a pound. When guests in the 1960s questioned the standard Duck's charge of fifty-two cents for a beer that would have cost them twenty cents in Jacksonville, the reply was, "This is a resort area, and it costs more to bring you the product here."

The employees'-eye view of Duck's offers some impressive details. At least a dozen workers—Davis family members and a number of high school and college students—served from the main dining room, side porch, and patio, with room service available for the church people who valued their privacy. No one outworked the Davis family itself. Alonzo Davis was the top chef. His parents, Mother D and Pop, saw that the larder and coolers were well stocked and kept tight control of the inventory. Pauline Davis, who

Shipping shrimp from Fernandina dock, 1957. Restaurateurs drove their trucks to the docks early in the morning to haul away their orders. Locals stopped by the docks when the boats arrived and picked up the throwaways. Over the years, the shrimpers have provided many free crab boils and fish fries to the islanders. Courtesy Florida State Archives.

had worked at the Afro Pavilion since she was a teenager, served as concierge.

One of the students was Mike Phelts, who worked at Duck's every summer. He drove the pickup truck into Fernandina on Thursdays for the weekend order and on Monday to replenish supplies for the week.[4] At the docks he shopped for fresh seafood, buying a hundred pounds of fish per visit, fifty pounds of shrimp, and several pounds of crabmeat. Back at the inn, the shrimp had to be peeled and deveined, dipped in an egg batter and seasoned, then laid in trays, stack upon stack, and frozen. The fish, though cleaned at the docks, had to be seasoned, coated with meal, and individually quick frozen. Over extended holiday weekends, the fish seldom hit the freezer. They were prepped straight from the number-two size tin tubs, seasoned, and plopped into the fryer. Huge boxes of whole fresh chickens arrived from the poultry market in Jacksonville every Friday morning to be cut up, seasoned, then refrigerated. When an order for chicken came through, the chicken was dipped in a batter made from Golden Dip Batter Mix, milk, and eggs, and plunged in the hot oil of the deep fryer. On long, crowd-swelling weekends, chicken and fish sold out.

When the buses rolled in from the other southeastern states, Duck's burst at the seams. As soon as the diesel engines reverberated along Lewis Street, the crews at Ducks and other restaurants geared up for their day. Mike Phelts began in the kitchen as the breakfast short-order cook, sliding grits onto the burner, then stacking smoked sausages on the low-fired grill. Next, he filled the coffee urn and cracked dozens of eggs he would scramble as orders came in. He turned on the deep fryer at a low temperature, waiting for the first breakfast order of fish and grits.

Later, with the cooking fires burning for the chef, Phelts moved on to busing tables, washing dishes, and cleaning the dining rooms and bathrooms, in preparation for the steady stream of customers. His most challenging job on weekends, when all three dining rooms were in service, was having enough clean china. Sometimes the cook had up to five orders ready to go with no dishes to put them on, while the plates were being bused from the tables to the sink.

After twenty years at American Beach, Alonzo Davis retired as Duck's inn-keeper in 1972 and returned to Jacksonville.

The inn closed in the late 1980s. The building is now the beach home of its last proprietor, Cora Davis (no relation to the Alonzo Davis family), who lives there with her family and on occasion accommodates weddings, reunions, and private parties. In 1994 her daughter, Janet, returned to the beach from Washington, D.C., bought additional property, and began renovating Duck's with plans for opening a club on American Beach where the sounds of jazz would resonate once again.

CHAPTER 8

A Who's Who of Vacationers and Visitors

I don't like money actually, but it quiets my nerves.
JOE LOUIS

Roadside trees swayed and bowed in the storm of sand and dust kicked up by the Greyhound buses and yellow-hound school buses that rumbled into American Beach from the 1930s to the early 1970s, carrying excursion groups from everywhere in the southeast. On holiday weekends the buses lined Lewis Street for the quarter mile from highway A1A to the beach. Even the affordable motels that sprang up during the late 1940s and early 1950s would buckle under the demand. As the inn and motels filled, proprietors contacted homeowners throughout the community to take in the overflow. In cottages and trailers, guests moved into extra bedrooms or onto porches, where they were assigned to cots and chaise lounges for beds. These were the heydays of American Beach, a tourist mecca that guaranteed African Americans a good time.

COMPANY PERKS: THE AFRO'S CABINS AND PICNICS

The Afro kept six cabins for the exclusive use of families of company executives and employees. Each summer as perquisites for outstanding service and salesmanship, the Afro gave their top salespersons free use of these cabins for one or two weeks. Each had a large front porch, a closed-in back porch, a garage, two bedrooms, a living room, a kitchen, a bathroom, and a view of the ocean.

Robert Stewart, director of agents for the Afro, spent two weeks at the end of each summer in one of these cabins with his family. With only a two-burner kerosene stove in the cabin, the Stewarts brought to the beach with them baked cakes, the electric pot that 103-year-old Ruth Stewart cooks on even today, and a ham to be boiled in the pot for sandwiches through the week. They bought vegetables by the bushel from a stand on the way into Fernandina. Catching crabs at low tide was a popular family activity. The incoming tide dug out sloughs, stranding crabs, shrimp, and fish when it retreated, and the Stewarts picked up crabs by the bucket fulls. In the evenings everybody sat around the dinner table and picked crab meat. They ate crab cakes for breakfast, crab salad for lunch, fish stew or gumbo for dinner.[1]

Family and friends of Afro employees enjoy the American Beach playground while vacationing in company cabins, 1939. Left to right: Nolan Gaines, Ernestine McCain Bazzell, James Bazzell, Gwendolyn Hunter (Witsell), Edward Witsell, Saramae Stewart, and Julian Foster. Courtesy Saramae Stewart Richardson.

Besides vacations at the beach, Stewart's widow, Ruth, remembers the company's many perks, such as higher salaries, bonuses, and opportunities to become shareholders, which allowed her to stay at home and be a homemaker. Ordinarily a woman with a college degree was expected to be employed in some respected position, but wives of Afro executives rarely worked outside the home. Also, the company employed their children and other family members. Ruth Stewart recalled that executives' families each year received a huge turkey for Christmas from the Afro's Model Farm in Madison.[2] The Stewarts, as well as many other Afro families, also had the opportunity to invest in the company.

During A. L. Lewis's presidency, the company held elaborate Fourth of July picnics at the beach, a tradition that had its beginning in Franklin Town before the company acquired American Beach in 1935. Lewis enlisted a host of capable people for their culinary services. Philanthropist Douglas Anderson, for whom a prestigious performing arts high school in Jacksonville is named, provided the bus transportation to the picnics. Lewis called upon Fernandina businessman Robert M. Ellerson to do the barbecuing. (Ellerson was known for his boat excursions and organizing huge Emancipation Day parades. He was also a business partner of Miss Martha's husband, Lemuel Hippard.) After Ellerson's death in 1936, Walter Lancaster, a chef on the railroad, catered the company picnics from 1937 through the 1960s.

The picnics were a holiday all their own, recalls longtime Afro employee Bernice Griffin.[3] Every employee was given the day off to celebrate. The Afro provided transportation, and there was as much food as you could eat: barbecued chicken and ribs, tubs of potato salad, and hot, fresh-fried fish. The Stewart children, Saramae Richardson and James Stewart, remembered in the 1930s the men seining along the shore, then hauling to the picnic site tubs filled with just-caught jumbo shrimp, meaty crabs, and fish. Company executives fried the fish on the site, and the people ate it as fast as they could cook it. Soft drinks and lemonade were served from a specially built oasis with a palmetto-leaf roof, constructed by the men in the middle of the broad field behind the oceanfront homes of Lewis and Louis Dargan Ervin.

After the elder Lewis's death in 1947, a second beach celebration was added to celebrate the birthday of company president James H. Lewis in July; the company picnic followed at the end of the beach season, shortly after Labor Day.

Griot Ruth Stewart with Afro president James H. Lewis and Dennis Stewart, 1951. The three structures in the background are Afro cabins. Courtesy Ruth Stewart.

When Willie Evans, owner of Evans's Rendezvous, began catering the end-of-season picnics during their final decade, he kept huge pans of beans baking slowly all the night before at his restaurant, while his crew prepared vats of cole slaw. Fried chicken had replaced fried fish as the main course, and Evans's employees were kept frying chicken all through the day for the picnickers. For the president, James H. Lewis, and his circle of friends, Evans roasted legs of lamb and prepared Lewis's favorite dishes, shrimp purlo and souse. (Evans describes souse as being like hog head cheese, except with more vinegar added to give the loaf a more sour taste.) Insurance company agents from as far away as Texas attended this event.

During its boom era, American Beach became a vibrant melting pot of African American culture. Although the Afro originally developed it as a playground for well-to-do employees and shareholders, the company also sold beachfront and near-beachfront lots to other elites.

Physicians, morticians, attorneys, professors, educators, railroad workers, entrepreneurs, and insurance and business executives built vacation homes there. The farther people traveled to vacation at the beach, the longer they stayed. Families of homeowners often spent the entire summer on the beach.

But by 1940, with fewer than twenty-five of the more than two hundred lots from the first thirty-three-acre tract sold, the Afro began a vigorous campaign to sell more lots. Whole 50-x-125-foot lots on Gregg Street right across from the ocean sold for $150. Now blue-collar workers too could buy property in the dream, taking their recreation alongside the privileged.

An impressive who's who could be developed from those who have vacationed on American Beach. During the summer of 1939, the folklorist and writer Zora Neale Hurston, then living in Jacksonville and working for the Works Project Administration, came to the beach and collected stories from the Drummonds and other Franklin Town families. That was the summer she married a fellow WPA colleague, Albert W. Price III, one of Jacksonville's most handsome and well-to-do young bachelors. Price was the grandson of a founder and former president of the Afro-American Life Insurance Company, A. W. Price Sr. His family had been major shareholders and employees in the company; his grandmother was on the board of directors. Albert was twenty-three years old and Hurston forty-eight when they crossed the Nassau County line to apply for a license and take their vows on June 27.[4]

Hurston joined the church of her husband's family, Bethel Baptist Institutional, where her brother John Hurston was a deacon.[5] For a short while they lived in the Price family home next door to the church where Price's grandfather's name is inscribed as a founding trustee. Although people in Jacksonville say that Zora was crazy about Price—and so did she in her autobiography, *Dust Tracks on a Road*—only seven months after the wedding she filed for divorce in Duval County.[6] Both she and Price obtained Afro attorneys to represent them. Hurston's lawyer was Samuel Decatur McGill, who at the time he represented her won a U.S. Supreme Court decision for the freedom of the Pompano Boys, who had spent nine years

Afro stenographers enjoying the 1969 beach picnic. Left to right: Dorothy Wilson, Audrey McCray, Ruth Thomas. Courtesy Ruth Thomas.

on Florida's death row for a murder they didn't commit. Price was represented by J. Leonard Lewis, the grandson of A. L. Lewis, who became president of the Afro upon the death of A. W. Price Sr.

There have been many other renowned visitors to American Beach's shores. Billie Daniels, famous for his song "That Old Black Magic," was a Jacksonville native whose family still owns property on the beach. Other prominent annual vacationers during the 1940s and 1950s were Cab Calloway, Ray Charles, Billy Eckstein, Hank Aaron, and Joe Louis. A frequent guest of N. E. Fluker has been his Waycross, Georgia, childhood friend, the actor Ossie Davis.

On his rise to fame in the early 1950s, rhythm-and-blues singer James Brown came to American Beach to put on an outdoor concert at Evans's Rendezvous. But Evans wouldn't hear of Brown's plan to rope off the outside of his business to sell tickets for an oceanside performance—he feared the crowd on the beach would draw from his business inside the Rendezvous. Evans sent Brown and his manager looking for another audience.

The list of well-known visitors and residents continues today. Television

Crowds returned to American Beach in the 1980s to find that Amelia Island Plantation surrounded the area of ocean wilderness. Condos in the background of this 1985 photo are evidence of the development of the shoreline. Courtesy Henry Lee Adams Jr.

Atlanta jazz musician Sam Anderson's twilight saxophone serenade during the annual Virgo Bash, 1991. Courtesy Michael Stewart.

Actress Barbara Montgomery, flanked in this 1992 photo by Sabrin Rosier and Sabrin's grandmother, Eva R. Lamar. Courtesy Michael Phelts.

Edna Calhoun, reflecting on the life of Reverend E. J. Gregg, founding president of the Afro-American Industrial and Benefit Association in 1901, at the 1995 Founders' Day celebration on American Beach. Courtesy James Robinson.

Jazz drummer Billy Moore plays for the Arlington Elementary School PTA, January 30, 1991, with the help of (from left) students Sinamon Larracunte on the scratcher, Elaina Washington on the shaker, Amanda Savell on the go-go bells, and Mathew Witcher on the claves. Moore is a member of Atlanta's African-American Philharmonic Orchestra and has played with a number of jazz greats. Courtesy Ronald W. Bayless, Florida Publishing Company.

and film actress Barbara Montgomery purchased a vacation home at the beach through the encouragement of her friend, Sarah Allen, a former actress and mother of tennis star Leslie Allen. Many of Montgomery's TV and stage friends have joined her at her American Beach retreat. Sarah Allen also influenced singer and dramatist Alexander Hickson and the late portrait and landscape artist Bradley Phillips to purchase homes and property on American Beach. During the summer, Alexander Hickson directs weekly oceanside reader's theater programs for islanders and visiting artists-in-residence.

Having lived and worked at Howard University in Washington, D.C., for many years, Dean Edna Calhoun—daughter of Mt. Zion AME Church pastor John Calhoun—returned to American Beach in the mid 1980s.

American Beach has always been a vacation home to international percussionist and jazz drummer Billy Lionel Moore and his brother Allan Moore Jr. (When Billy made his debut at Carnegie Hall on May 8, 1966, his mother, a professional musician, did not know that her son was performing until the curtain rose upon him at center stage. For moments the only sound was the hard rapid clapping of Alpha Moore's hands as she sprang from her seat saying, "Thank you Jesus! Thank you Jesus!")[7]

U.S. federal judge Henry Lee Adams Jr. and his family have been beach residents for decades. Adams served as president of the local civic and preservation group, American Beach, Inc., in 1990-91, when an annual Labor Day Awards Program was initiated, a popular event that recognizes individuals for public and community services beneficial to American Beach. Florida Supreme Court justice Leander Shaw and his family are neighbors of the Adams, and county judge James Ruth also shares a home with his family on American Beach.

Elaine Adams, wife of federal judge Henry Adams Jr., in search of red bass in 1992. Hooking a big red usually marks the can't-beat-that end of a fishing expedition and motivates those nearby to try and reel in the next one. Courtesy Henry Adams.

A 1950s Trip to the Beach

The shores of the great river, full of promises, / Henceforth belong to you.
PATRICE LUMUMBA

When I was a child, the highlight of every summer's vacation was our retreat to American Beach for two weeks in July. We loaded up our baby
blue, two-door 1950 Ford, Old Betsy, and headed out Main Street in Jacksonville to drop off our dogs, Duke and Duchess, at the kennel. Across the
Main Street Bridge, Old Betsy would make a right turn by the Jacksonville
Zoo on Heckscher Drive, and for the next thirty miles we sped east toward
the ocean over one bridge right after another—a dozen between the Main
Street Bridge and the beach.

My brothers and I held our breath as Old Betsy made her way up,
around, and over Dead Man's Curve. Coming out of the curve, we approached Drummond Point, where we crossed the bridge at the Eastport
peninsula; then we crossed the concrete Dunn Creek Bridge through the
New Berlin peninsula. At Brown Creek we crossed the bridge to another
island, and from Cedar Point Creek, we drove through Marsh Island and
over Hannah Mills Creek to Pine Island. We closed our eyes tight and crossed
all our fingers as we clippity-cloppity rumbled over the wooden swaying

My mother and father, Eva and Charles Rosier, in 1941. My love for the beach grew from theirs. In our family, American Beach was the unanimous vacation choice. Courtesy Eva Lamar.

bridges at Clap Board Creek and Sisters Creek, praying hard that our car would not plunge through the missing planks. The raggedy boards in the bridges sounded a loud plonk, plonk, plonk. After the Sisters Creek Bridge, our last wooden bridge, we were on Flanning Island. Soon we would see the ocean.

We drove quickly through Pilot Town, the harbor village of the boat pilots and their families, and sped past the Buccaneer Ferry Slip, where the ferry transported vehicles and pedestrians across the channel to Mayport. Soon we were on Batten Island, then Fort George Island. We approached the mouth of the Fort George Inlet, where the St. Johns River and its tributaries reached the end of their watery 372-mile journey north and gushed into the sea. From the bridge over to Little Talbot Island we caught our first glimpse of the Atlantic, bursting from its bed in wave upon wave, pound-

Contestants for the title of Miss American Beach, 1958. Courtesy Eartha White Collection, University of North Florida Library, Jacksonville.

ing against concrete boulders, then retreating. From this point, it was ocean all the way—dunes, surf, towering pine and palm trees around each bend in the twisting and winding Buccaneer Trail that led to American Beach and the A. L. Lewis Motel.

By the 1950s, American Beach was an entrepreneur's dream. Owners of lodgings and restaurants were expanding services to accommodate travelers from twenty-nine of the forty-eight states. Upon arrival on the American Beach playground, guests had lots of activities and amusements to engage in, including beauty pageants for children and young adults. Families who took annual vacations at the beach often secured reservations for the next season before they returned home. The new masonry ranch-style A. L. Lewis Motel, with twenty-two luxuriously equipped units, opened to the public in 1950. The Pension Bureau of the Afro-American Life Insurance Company spent in excess of $125,000 to construct and furnish this modern facility, according to its 1965 reservations brochure.

For us, going to American Beach was the equivalent of going to Disney World today, in terms of its popularity and prestige. It was a place where dreams came true just by being there, the place for family gatherings or community get-togethers, the place to see and gape at the prominent personalities of the community.

At the motel, we quickly unloaded Betsy; there was still lots of daylight left, so we always went in the water on our first day. If we had made reservations a summer in advance, we would have corner unit number one or twenty-two—the whole family, and sometimes our extended family, stayed there. We preferred number twenty-two because it was the farthest from the watchful eye of the manager, Mrs. Holley, in unit six, for at no time did we have fewer than five people staying in a unit meant for four. The corner units, with two extra windows, each rented for seven dollars a day, the inside units for six.

Each unit was fully furnished with bath, kitchen, and bed linens, cookware, silverware, dishes, glasses—everything but an electric fan. They weren't

Charles Jr., Marsha, and Kenneth Rosier, at the May 1954 sixth-grade graduation ceremony at Susie E. Tolbert Elementary School in Jacksonville. Courtesy Eva Lamar.

American Beach Villas, the former A. L. Lewis Motel, in 1992. At ebb tide, the Villas lies only some three hundred feet from the ocean's ripples. Courtesy Michael Phelts.

air-conditioned; it was a rare home or business that had air-conditioning in the 1950s. Our front door and windows stayed open the whole time we were there, welcoming sea breezes and the fresh-mollusk island smells of the sea and shore.

Every meal at the beach became a treat; favorite foods that were limited privileges at home appeared on the menu by request. We drank Kool-Aid for breakfast, lunch, and dinner—iced tea only if we wanted it. At the beach we made Kool-Aid with sulfur water, which gave it an extra kick. The only other times we had sulfur water were when we went to the zoo or visited our relatives in the country. (Many people disliked sulfur water and said that it had the smell and taste of rotten eggs, but our family savored the taste of sulfur-water beverages.) We also brought to the beach with us a case of assorted soda water: Nehi orange, grape, and strawberry, and pineapple soda water too. Nothing tasted so good to us in those hot summer, un-air-conditioned days as homemade honey drippers made from Kool-Aid or soda. Before we went to bed at night we put paper cups of Kool-Aid or soda in the freezer to be ready for the next day. This was like making a popsicle in a cup.

In the mornings before breakfast, we got crab nets and a bucket, scampered to the beach in search of little sand mounds at the surf, and dug for big blue crabs and speckled crabs. In tidal pools we scooped up crab after crab; we needed no bait. Mullets were a different matter. We ran and scooped time after time, trying to catch the minnowlike, lightning-fast fish. At low tide, we delighted in filling our sieve with donax, tiny colorful coquina clams, easy to gather by the thousands as they lay on top of the sand—purple, orange, blue, yellow, pink, and white. After slurping bowls of donax broth, we used the shells to create mosaics on driftwood or poster board to take back home.

Evenings found us in front of the motel playing shuffleboard or croquet and marveling at the Blue Palace and its goings on directly in front of the motel. This splendid structure, built in 1951 by Dr. and Mrs. Robert M. Harris of Atlanta, was a two-story mansion built of concrete blocks and painted baby blue, naturally backed by the blues of ocean and sky. The windows and door facings were trimmed with glass bricks that reflected sunbeams throughout the day, while interior lights and moonbeams made them sparkle through the night. At the ground-level approach to the entrance, steps curved like amphitheater seats ran the full width of the home. In the middle of this magnificent structure was a garage with a drive that went straight through to the ocean. I did not know the Harris family, but from my perch at the motel, I spent many hours a day dreaming of life in the Blue Palace, and many evening hours gazing at the elegant people invited to soirees there.

At the end of two weeks of American Beach sun, my brothers and I would crowd in front of the bathroom mirror—to inspect each other and agree on who was the beach blackest.

CHAPTER 10

Hurricane Dora

The wind came back with triple fury, and put out the light for the last time.
ZORA NEALE HURSTON

The Thursday after Labor Day, September 10, 1964, Hurricane Dora blew into American Beach from the west coast of Africa and invaded the Blue Palace, smashing and crashing through every room, snatching furniture, glass, fixtures, concrete blocks, doors, gates, fences, and carrying them out to sea. She also pulled several entire houses from their foundations and swept them into the ocean, although a few were later recovered.

OPEN HOUSE AT THE BLUE PALACE

When Dora ended her rendezvous on American Beach, she left the once graceful Blue Palace in shambles; it was never again occupied or restored. For thirty years, the ruins were a subject for photographers, artists, and happy snappers, a conversation piece for beach strollers, and an accommodating hostess to picnickers or squatters.

The last picture painted by portrait and landscape artist Bradley S. Phillips of New York and American Beach was of the Blue Palace. American Beach,

The Blue Palace after taking a blow from the winds and water of Hurricane Dora, September 11, 1964. Courtesy Lyndon Godwin.

Inc., paid tribute to Bradley's contribution with a resolution passed during the tenure of Henry Adams Jr.:

AMERICAN BEACH, FLORIDA

Whereas, Bradley S. Phillips a distinguished portrait and landscape painter was a resident of Greenwich Village in New York; and
Whereas, Bradley S. Phillips was also a resident of American Beach on Amelia Island, Florida where he adored the people and was intrigued with the island's splendor; and
Whereas, the people of American Beach responded to Bradley's warmth, welcoming him with friendship and respect; and
Whereas, the years that Bradley shared his life with us on American Beach were only five, his presence and contributions have been immortalized; and
Whereas, Bradley S. Phillips' last painting was that of the Blue Palace on American Beach; and
Whereas, the Blue Palace once renowned for its majestic beauty before Hurricane Dora in 1964, it continues to be awed by many as remnants of a glorious era now in ruins; and

Whereas, Bradley S. Phillips' painting of the Blue Palace epitomizes his love of American Beach and will be a lasting tribute to this beach's rich legacy of people of color; and

Whereas, on one day the walls and sight of the Blue Palace will be visible to us no more, Bradley S. Phillips and the great Blue Palace will live long after their physical presence have been forgotten:

Whereas, "For every joy that passes, something beautiful remains."

Now, Therefore, let it be resolved that Bradley S. Phillips' life and works will be remembered long after his demise on May 1, 1991.

Presented to Bradley's family In Memoriam: A Celebration of the Life of Bradley S. Phillips on this 16th day of June 1991.

American Beach, Inc.

Henry Lee Adams, Jr., President
Marsha Dean Phelts, Secretary

In 1993, the seven Dawkins brothers and their wives and their parents Wilbert and Tinye bought the ruins of the Blue Palace. As it was past restoring, on April 15, the remainder of the house was demolished; huge dump trucks hauled away the rubble. The new owners, Dr. and Mrs. Wilbert

Hurricane Dora ravaging the shores of Amelia Island, September 9, 1964. Courtesy Florida Publishing Company.

Dawkins of Jacksonville and their sons, then constructed a grand landmark of their own. The Dawkins family built their 1,800-square-foot beach home on concrete pilings—building codes had changed long since the days when the Blue Palace was constructed. Fernandina architect Bud Coe designed the eclectic Mediterranean home, providing each room with an open view of the ocean and constructed a balcony all the way across the second story.

DAMAGE AT THE RENDEZVOUS AND WILLIAMS'S LODGE

Dora not only destroyed the Blue Palace but rearranged American Beach and affected the whole of Florida's northeast coast. Evans's Rendezvous proprietor Willie Evans said that the building felt as if it were leaning, as Dora howled for hours throughout the night. The hurricane swept the ocean three hundred feet from its watery bed and across Gregg Street to rest in the restaurant's parking lot, ripped off the entire front of the Rendezvous porch, pulled out bathroom fixtures, and carried out to sea seven freezers filled with fish and other meats.[1] Dora also wreaked havoc on the two-story concrete structure next door that housed Tino's Restaurant and wiped out three cabins in front of Tino's as if they had never been there. The next day, Evans saw his freezers floating like boats in the ocean.

On the northernmost end of the beach, Dora struck another community landmark, Williams's Guest Lodge. Moses Lewis Williams, a grocer in Jacksonville, his wife, Illinois (known as Tillie), and their daughters, Mozella and Ruth, had built a summer cottage on the beach in 1945, a weekend retreat from their store. Not long afterward, when neighborhood groceries began having trouble competing with the lower prices of the new, larger chain grocery stores like Daylight Grocery and Setzer's, Williams took his wife's suggestion that he operate a motel and restaurant on the beach. He bought oceanfront property from their Jacksonville neighbor, George E. Curry, a bishop of the African Methodist Episcopal Church and a professor at Edward Waters College.[2]

Williams himself built the lodge from the ground up in 1949, a beautiful, durable oceanfront structure, using the best building materials. Williams's Guest Lodge was patronized by the black elite, among them college and university presidents—Frederick D. Patterson of Tuskegee Institute, George Gore of Florida A & M University, and the King family from Atlanta University. (Dr. Patterson worked with A. L. Lewis and the Afro in the efforts to successfully acquire the parcel of oceanfront property for American Beach

Evans's Rendezvous after Dora. Many structures along the oceanfront collapsed to rubble from the force of the hurricane. Courtesy Lyndon Godwin.

from the federal government.) Executives from *Ebony* and *Jet* magazines vacationed at Williams's, and so did hundreds of prominent area and regional citizens.

In this family-operated business, the Williamses prepared and served seafood to perfection—Tillie's savory fried shrimp earned a reputation—and the dining room was filled to capacity most nights. The cleanliness and freshness of the lodge made it inviting; the hospitality and warmth that the family extended made it irresistible. A special amenity was the electric fan in every room. At other lodging facilities, patrons had to rent fans for a dollar a day. Williams's thirteen suites were filled with guests who stayed two and three weeks at a time, and many prolonged their vacations beyond Labor Day.[3]

On September 9, 1964, the lodge was full when the order came to evacuate the beach due to the approaching storm. Those who could took inland routes home. Four families could not leave for their homes on the East Coast and had to ride out the storm at the Williams home in Jacksonville.

Throughout the day and into the night of September 10, Hurricane Dora came roaring up the shore. The waters from the ocean rapidly rose over the dunes and tore into Williams's Guest Lodge, smashing windows, bashing down doors, ripping off the porch, and carrying out to sea furnishings, concrete walls, the deep freeze, pots, pans, and dishes. On that same day, Mrs. Williams suffered a heart attack. While she was hospitalized, her neighbors salvaged what provisions and furnishings they could from the Williams's larder and boarded up the building.

In 1967, Mrs. Williams suffered a second, fatal heart attack. For a few years afterwards, Mr. Williams, with the help of his daughter, Ruth McCaskill, continued operating the lodge. Today, the building has long been leveled into the dunes.[4]

Before Dora, storms usually hit American Beach at the end of summer, and beachgoers returning for the next season never knew what the beach had weathered. Home and property owners had made the necessary repairs and restorations in time to open for business in May. Dora was different. Residents talk about that hurricane as if it happened last year rather than three decades ago. When they hear about a storm brewing from the coast of Africa en route to the northeast coast of Florida, they offer fervent prayers that it not come ashore on American Beach.

CHAPTER 11

Gay Poppers, Boomerangs, and High Fashion at the Crossroads

*There are roads out of the secret place within us along which
we must all move as we go to touch others.*
ROMARE BEARDEN

At the crossroads of Lewis and Gregg Streets, where the rhythms of "Zing
Went the Strings of My Heart" and "Lonely Teardrops" played from juke-
boxes in American Beach's golden era, today the rap sounds of L. L. Cool J
and Snoop Doggy Dogg thump from amplified car stereos and boom boxes.
Instead of the dazzling neon lights that beckoned passersby to clubs in years
past, bright streaks of violet, magenta, teal, green, and orange glow from
four-wheel-drive jeeps and trucks parading at dusk, and cars resurrected
from the 1950s and 1960s spring and dip to the beat, moving slowly through
the crossroads with girls sitting on their fenders. But while the trappings
may have changed, the motive hasn't. Since the beginning, everyone at American Beach has passed through, gathered, or lingered at the intersection of
Lewis and Gregg Streets, the grand entrance to the Atlantic Ocean, to see
and to be seen.

Approaching the crossroads from Lewis Street and Ocean Boulevard: a place to see and be seen. Courtesy Henry Lee Adams Jr.

El Patio

In the early fifties, finger-popping good times jumped from all corners of the crossroads, where teenagers danced the sawdust floor from under their feet at El Patio on the northwest corner. El Patio started as an open-air partition square, built by Clifford Swint from South Carolina to cater to the younger crowd, then in the early 1960s expanded to cover the full length of the block by its present owner, Elizabeth Simmons Jones. From El Patio's juke boxes, or piccolos, the top tunes of the day boomed around the clock, ten cents for a single, three for a quarter, seven for fifty cents. The big main piccolo stood against a middle wall in the club's main room, and each of the booths that lined the walls had a table-top piccolo connected to the main player.

For ten cents you could hear the Coasters sing "Searching" or "Youngblood" or Etta James croon "The Love of My Man," which brought the whole house to the dance floor to do the slow drag. Tunes by Ruth Brown, Ben E. King, and the Drifters tugged at the hearts of teenagers as poignantly as the moon shining on the ocean.

Even with a block-long building, dancing crowds from El Patio spilled out onto the streets. The dance floor was not large enough to hold all the gay poppers—slang for "good timers" or "a group of people having a social good time." During the summer of 1959 a dance called the John Price that swept the nation began in Jacksonville and on American Beach, performed by a fellow named John Price, who rode its popularity onto the national rhythm-and-blues circuit.

Just around the corner from El Patio was Reynold's Sandwich Shop, a stopover for those trying to squeeze their way into Evans's Rendezvous. Fish sandwiches and beer were popular items. Walter Reynolds, the proprietor, had relocated to the South from New York. He drove cabs in Jacksonville during the winter and operated his sandwich shop during beach season. It was a small shop on a quarter lot, built during the beach's early years when county building codes were more than lenient.

The Guess House behind the Sweet Tooth

Across Gregg Street from El Patio, atop a dune on the northeast corner of the crossroads, the Sweet Tooth sold huge puffs of cotton candy and swirling ice cream cones too tall to eat before they melted. A little quieter than the other corners, the Sweet Tooth was a family ice cream parlor where children could watch the cotton candy spun before their eyes in huge copper vats. The sweet-cooked pink smells wafted through the salt air throughout the days and into the evenings.

A few feet east of the Sweet Tooth stood the Guess House, a little wooden makeshift jail for processing those charged with misdemeanors or felonies, where the accused had the choice of paying cash bonds or taking a trip to the jail downtown. Deputies called the Nassau County Jail the Guess House, short for "Guess when you're getting out?"

Sometimes it seemed it didn't take much to be sent to the Guess House—just go to Nassau County and pass through roadblocks set up on American Beach. These roadblocks gave deputies the opportunity to search cars, detain lawbreakers, and confiscate booze and other contraband. But Lieutenant Tim Alberta says that for the twenty-five years he has been in county law enforcement, the sheriff's office has served the beach well: "If we weren't here doing what we do, keeping our eyes out for knives and guns in past decades, to automatic weapons and cocaine today, we'd all have been run off the beach."

Alberta talked about the bus that used to come in from a Jacksonville club every weekend driven by a fellow known as Cut Price. On show night at Evans's Rendezvous, when the female impersonators filled the place to capacity, Cut Price had a lot of trouble from his riders when the time came for them to go back to Jacksonville. "There have been times during the 1970s when things got so rowdy we had to arrest the whole busload," Alberta said. "They'd get down here, drinking that liquor, enjoying the shows in Evans's, and, when it was time to board the bus heading back to Jacksonville, they'd break out in a big brawl."[1] Many times Cut Price himself had to signal the police to pull his bus off the road and load up the paddy wagons with bottle-busting, cursing rabble-rousers. Sometimes the entire bus was escorted to the jail.

THE BOOMERANGS FROM JACKSONVILLE

Lieutenant Alberta remembered the Boomerangs' buses, too. It didn't take the deputies long to get acquainted with this 1960s gang from Jacksonville, which didn't tolerate passage through their neighborhood in the heart of town. Blacks who lived on either side of Jacksonville had to cross Boomerang territory to go to the Jefferson Street Swimming Pool, the only pool for blacks in the city, or to a movie at one of the three black movie theaters, the Ritz, Roosevelt, and Strand Theater, or simply to go downtown shopping.

Certain trouble lay in store for any young fellow who tried to talk to a Boomerette, a girlfriend of a Boomerang member. My schoolmate Barbara Warren, a high-stepping majorette at Stanton High School, was not just a Boomerette but the girlfriend of the gang's leader. During her recent class reunion on American Beach, she reminisced about the bus trips that the Boomerangs sponsored to the beach during the summers in the early 1960s.[2] Before heading for the shore, their chartered yellow-hound buses picked up gang members and friends from the Blodgett Home Projects and from such streets as Dewdrop Lane, Court J, Caroline, and other notorious streets in Jacksonville's black bottom.

On American Beach the Boomerangs set off altercations and disturbances in clubs and raised plenty of sand in the dunes. It got so that as soon as their bus pulled up in the parking lot, deputies would be over to check them coming off the bus. When a deputy spotted a Hawk Bill knife sticking out of some gang member's pocket, he had just cause to search the entire bus. Often the deputies found additional knives and guns, and—to their surprise—marijuana. Weekend after weekend the Boomerangs turned the beach out with fracases. Deputies soon began arresting Boomerangs before they started trouble. When the gang members abandoned the bus and began coming to the beach in cars, the deputies already knew them and kept after them, until the Boomerangs finally left American Beach in peace.

RENDEZVOUS AT THE CROSSROADS

Anyone lucky enough to find a parking place in the lot on the southwest corner of Lewis and Gregg turned their automobile, truck, motorcycle, chartered bus, or motor home into a social headquarters. Barbecue grills were fired up all over, sending appetizing aromas through the air. During World War II, when soldiers on horseback patrolled the coastline, the parking lot was government property, a barracks for soldiers and marines. Pauline Exson Davis, who during the war worked at the Casino in the Afro Pavilion, yelled across to the barracks to notify soldiers of their messages or phone calls.[3] During the golden era of American Beach, James Lincoln Lewis, great-grandson of A. L. Lewis, operated the lot, which also served as an extended holding area for those watching and waiting for an opportunity to inch their

The parking lot across from Evans's Rendezvous has long been a popular spot for off-ocean tailgate parties and all sorts of recreational vehicles, buses, trucks, cars, and motorcycles. Courtesy Henry Lee Adams Jr.

way into Evans's Rendezvous. In 1981 the company sold the parking lot to Frank and Emma Morgan, who still operate it today.

At the southeast corner of Lewis and Gregg, with its main entrance facing the parking lot, stood the king of the crossroads, Evans's Rendezvous, a landmark that has endeared American Beach to thousands. Among them were many students from Georgia and Florida who treasure their after-the-prom memories spent at the beach. Ben Darby and Earl Harris, Stanton High School class of 1960, came to the beach in tails and tuxedos, their prom dates on their arms in long laced and ruffled gowns. After dinner at the Duck Inn, with their high-heeled satin shoes in hand, the girls strutted barefoot next to their dates down Lewis Street, on to Evans's Rendezvous for a fish sandwich and a good time as they wore the night away to daybreak.

All sorts of flamboyant fashion styles were strutted at the crossroads on Sundays. Many people arrived straight from church on Sunday afternoons. When you spotted the churchgoers, you knew that either they were living under their parents' roof and the house rule was church first; or they didn't want to risk having to stay at home after returning from church for a change of clothes. On Sunday evenings, as the sun set over the Amelia River, the same dressed-for-church scenario was repeated, this time by deacons, elders, and sisters who raced to American Beach after evening worship to claim a spot at the crossroads for a refreshing repast and relaxation in the sea breezes.

When a summer evening at the crossroads got well fired up, music from the 45 rpm on Evans's piccolo would outblast the same song from the record on a piccolo in another establishment, and the atmosphere would reverberate with the music bouncing back and forth among the crossroads juke joints. There was no sleep for the American Beach community on those nights, as pop tunes rang through the darkness, backed by the spinning wheels of cars rolling in or rolling out.

CHAPTER 12

Evans's Rendezvous

They ate the whole fish. When empty plates came back to the kitchen,
even the eyeballs were gone.
WILLIE B. EVANS

From 1948 until 1980, a visitor might come to American Beach and never go in the water, but it seemed impossible that a visitor could come to American Beach and fail to go into Evans's Rendezvous. Huge floor fans vibrated constantly; windows and doors opened out to catch breezes. People poured in to Evans's by day and by night, partying through the night until nearly dawn. The atmosphere was electrifying, the excitement compelling. Anyone who lived within a fifty-mile radius and came to Evans's Friday or Saturday made it back the next day to recapture this magical feeling. Sometimes right in the middle of a superior evening, hundreds evacuated the place in moments because of the slash of a knife or a bottle smashing over someone's head after tempers flared or a case of too much brown liquor. Boasting that no one was ever killed in his place, Willie Evans added, "If somebody got shot, the people in the crowd had to move out the way to let them fall."[1]

Willie Evans first came to American Beach in 1940 on a Sunday excursion with the Civilian Conservation Corps from Folkston, Georgia. One of Franklin Roosevelt's New Deal government programs, the CCC hired young men for public conservation work during the Great Depression, and it existed until the United States entered World War II. On winter weekends, the Folkston CCC trucks drove black corps members over to Jacksonville to the movies; in the summer they brought them to American Beach, about sixty miles away. Evans was a cook for the CCC, and to make extra money he ran a shoeshine service on the side. He came from Orangeburg, South Carolina, where he had early training working and serving customers in his Uncle Herman's grocery store and gas station.

Impressed by American Beach and the crowds of people who gathered there, in 1941 Evans bought a little piece of beach property while he was still in the CCC. For $150, Lillie Rivers, the widow of Willie S. Rivers, sold him a 25-by-50-foot section, less than a quarter portion of her 50-by-125-foot lot. The piece faced the home of A. L. Lewis, where no smoking, drinking, or card playing was tolerated and where Lewis held Sunday school for beach residents on Sunday mornings, circumstances that would eventually work to Evans's benefit.

Willie B. Evans Sr., owner of Evans's Rendezvous from 1948 to 1980.

Evans enlisted the help of a fellow CCC recruit, Tom Blowers from Fernandina, who arranged for his father, a carpenter, to build the nice little jukek joint Evans had in mind. By the summer of 1942, Evans had a 22-by-42-foot structure on his partial lot, a yellow frame building with plenty of open windows to let in the light and breezes. He named it Sunny's Spot. At closing time, he secured the windows with batten planks of wood. During the day, he had to shoo out the goats who wandered in through the open doorway. Evans said that Lewis kept goats on the beach to get rid of the snakes.

The CCC was abolished in 1942, not long after the United States entered World War II, and the ex-CCC workforce provided the country with its first recruits. Evans was drafted on Thanksgiving Day 1942. For four years batten boards kept the sunlight out of Sunny's Spot while its owner was stationed in Illinois. When Evans returned to the beach after the war ended in 1946, folks were ready to celebrate. After one full summer of Sunny's Spot operating throughout the day and into the night directly across from the Lewis cottage, A. L. Lewis offered to exchange Evans's 25-by-50-foot ocean-view lot for a 50-by-150-foot oceanfront lot on the southern side of the beach, a piece of the eighty-three acres the Afro had just acquired from the government.

With the end of World War II, Gwendolyn Leapheart headed back to American Beach. This photo was taken during the summer of 1946. Courtesy Gwendolyn Leapheart.

School chums Mildred Hampton and Gwendolyn Leapheart partying on American Beach with a brand-new "let-back top" Oldsmobile that they borrowed from a fellow who was trying to impress another of their schoolmates. When it began to rain, the inside of the car was soaked because the girls didn't know to push the button to let up the top. Courtesy Gwendolyn Leapheart.

The only structure on the newly acquired property, which included 1,500 feet of ocean front, the new Sunny's Spot was a smashing success. A couple of years later, in order to accommodate the crowds that were pouring into his place, Evans moved the small building a half mile off the beach to the intersection of A1A near Stewart in Amelia City (Stewartville is a name coined to indicate the geographical area in which the Stewarts live). Renamed the Pirates Club, the building still stands there today, but it is not operating. Evans then built a two-story building and named it after himself.

THE RENDEZVOUS

At Evans's Rendezvous, people checked every fiber of social refinement at the door. If they were stepped on or over while gaining entrance or getting around—and they were—they didn't care. They stood three and four deep at the kitchen window or bar, inching their way to the cashier to place an order or waiting in a pack of pushing people to be served the next drink or delicious fish and chicken dinner. They bought hard liquor and beer by the bottle over the counter.

Customers whom Evans and his crew labeled big spenders started out paying for their liquor with twenty-dollar bills, buying Teacher's Scotch at four dollars a fifth. As the evening wore on, the bills that bought the rounds grew smaller and smaller. Toward the end, the orders changed from Scotch to wine, and the tab was paid with dollar bills and coins chipped in by everyone in the party. Evans and his staff provided guests with amenities right down to their last nickels and dimes. When parties began chipping in, it was a sure sign that the tables or booths could be bused and the next waiting group prepared to move in on the available space.

Although Evans's was the only establishment on American Beach with a liquor license, contraband liquor was available at many places, at higher prices, if the seller knew you. At Evans's, even though he sold liquor, many people from Jacksonville sneaked in their own liquor in big straw ladies' handbags. This didn't anger Evans, for a highly practical reason. "When you run out," he would think, "I've got you then; you can't go back to Jacksonville."

Evans's had a two-hundred-seat dining room and sold short orders and sandwiches. Short orders consisted of the entree served with lettuce and tomato salad, french fries, and buttered toast. The most popular items were fried fish and chicken. Customers could order from a variety of pan fish— whiting, mullet, trout, croakers, and spots—cleaned, split butterfly style,

View from the oceanfront porch of Evans's Rendezvous, ca. 1950. The most popular gathering place for dining and drinks on the beach was inside or on the front porch. The Rendezvous is one of the few remaining businesses on American Beach in the 1990s. Courtesy Ernestine Smith.

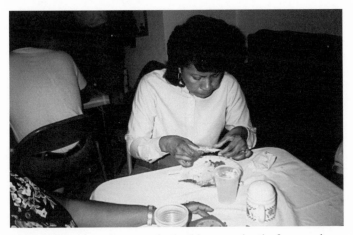

Mildred Sapp gets down to the backbone and tail of a succulent fried sea bass, 1992. Courtesy Michael Phelts.

and cooked whole in a frying pan. The fish most in demand, whiting, was fried and served whole from the head to the tail, backbone intact, every fin in place, eyeballs fried in the socket. What amazed Evans and his staff were the many fish dinner plates that returned to the kitchen with just a little pile on them that looked like sawdust—no bones, head, tail, fins, or even eyes.

The daytime crowds came to Evans's by the busload from Georgia and South Carolina and loaded back onto the buses by 4:30 in the afternoon, rolling out just as the Jacksonville crowds began rolling in near sundown. Many times this didn't give the crew a break to set up for the evening frolickers. Since Evans didn't have enough employees to provide for day and night shifts, the same staff that started in the morning kept on serving the crowds through the night.

In 1980, after nearly forty years of revelry, Willie Evans sold the Rendezvous to William Weathersbee, a retired high school football coach in Jacksonville. It is now the Ocean Rendezvous, where patrons can enjoy a summer Sunday afternoon as ocean breezes whirl through the room, propelled by vast electric fans. Coach Weathersbee presides at the bar, while handyman Tony Oliver dons his chef's hat and apron to fry fish dinners and short orders for those who remember when this was the place to be. The Rendezvous today bears no comparison to Evans's place, except that the ocean and memories remain.

CHAPTER 13

Sheriff H. J. Youngblood

*I can say one thing. I was sheriff for twenty-eight years and
was never called to Tallahassee to answer for any problems.*

H. J. YOUNGBLOOD

In 1932, Herbert J. Youngblood lost his first election for sheriff of Nassau
County by a single vote; he never lost another. His tenure lasted from 1941
through his retirement in January 1969. For more than a quarter of a century Youngblood's name and picture stared down from billboards across
the county's 649 square miles, and "H. J. Youngblood, Sheriff, Nassau County" was printed on every car in the sheriff's department, cruising reminders
to motorists on the county's three hundred miles of roads. Youngblood was
tall, and he wore a white, ten-gallon Stetson hat specially ordered from Texas
that made him look even taller.[1] The man in the white hat was both color-
blind and class blind. He ferreted out anyone violating a statute, black or
white, gamblers and moonshiners. One Sunday he and his posse walked
through Evans's Rendezvous out to the porch, picked up the money from
the table, and arrested Miss Martha and her gambling entourage.

The sheriff's law enforcement career began in 1915, when at twenty he
became superintendent of roads in Suwannee County, near Live Oak, a

Cap'n Herbert J. Youngblood and prison laborers, 1926. Youngblood is credited with constructing the backbone of the present Nassau County road system using prisoners and mules. Courtesy the Amelia Island Museum of History.

rural northwest Florida town. Five years later, he moved to Nassau County as head of the county road department, where he stood guard for twenty years as captain over chain gangs.[2] Bound with leg irons, the prisoners, aided by mules, felled trees and uprooted stumps to carve out hundreds of miles of county roads. Youngblood's cronies and subordinates and the chain gang all called him "Cap'n Youngblood."

TREATING PEOPLE RIGHT

Once Youngblood became sheriff, American Beach received a lot of attention from his deputies during the summer months. American Beach resident Captain Ben Sessions, a retired Nassau County deputy sheriff, recalled that Youngblood cautioned his deputies to treat people right. He also promised them, "If you stay alive, I'll protect you." Sessions worked the beat on American Beach, where the trouble spots for the deputies were less on the beaches themselves than at the hot spots for beachgoers—places at the cross-

For thirty years people paid to bail themselves out of the old jail in downtown Fernandina. Today they pay get in; the jail, shown here in a 1993 photo, is now home to the prestigious Amelia Island Museum of History. Courtesy Michael Phelts.

roads like Evans's Rendezvous and the parking lot. Deputies made frequent arrests for the possession of moonshine and guns, confiscating Smith & Wessons and shotguns by the sackful.[3]

The sand dunes overlooking the beach, rising sixty feet above sea level, offered deputies a different kind of crime. They watched amorous young couples climb the dunes until they disappeared over the other side, then ambled down, found them in compromising positions, and arrested them for indecent exposure. Other arrests were made for fights and disturbances, disorderly conduct, reckless driving, speeding—just about anything. People worried more about going to jail in Nassau County than they did about drowning in an undercurrent.

From 1935 to 1975, the two-story red-brick jail at 233 South Third Street in downtown Fernandina raked in the money through fines and bonds posted from the gay popping times on American Beach. Ad valorem taxes from the American Beach community more than paid for the services that the county made available to it. Annis Littles was a jail matron and a twenty-five-year employee of the sheriff's office. She cooked for those held overnight in jail and lived there with her husband, Bobby Moore, the chief deputy. Littles recalls that on Sundays at the old jail "there would be at least 150 arrests. Most of them were released on their own recognizance by the judge. Those that he didn't know from other counties usually spent a night in the jail to await a bond hearing."[4]

Riding the Youngblood Trail

The lawmen of Nassau County were notorious. To put it mildly, law and order in Sheriff Youngblood's northeast Florida fiefdom was perceived as unfair. Anyone who drove through its speed traps or roadblocks stood an extremely high chance of going to jail, especially if they weren't known to the deputies or somebody with clout.

For decades the only northern route to the beach from Jacksonville was a twenty-mile drive through Nassau County. After the MacArthur Toll Bridge was completed in 1952, Jacksonville motorists had another choice; the route through Heckscher Drive in Duval County was less likely to cause trouble with Nassau County law enforcement officials.

But Heckscher Drive was a narrow, curving, hilly, two-lane road that included a dangerous winding incline just past the Jacksonville zoo, Dead Man's Curve. Black motorists did not enjoy going out Main Street (US Highway 17) to Yulee, through Chester and O'Neal on to Fernandina down the Old Amelia Road to the American Beach turn-off. Nevertheless, African American beachgoers like my own family preferred the Buccaneer Trail—the Heckscher Drive route, with its natural obstacles—to the faster, smoother, less expensive Youngblood Trail, where their odds of running into Youngblood's deputies were greater—twenty-miles of Nassau County driving versus four miles via the toll-bridge route. When the Afro sponsored company picnics or other celebrations, A. L. Lewis arranged for the hiring of state troopers to escort motorists safely through the Youngblood Trail. Riding the Youngblood trail could be an expensive route for blacks.[5]

Jacksonville's John J. Coleman was a different story. Coleman ran fast cars and took whatever route he fancied. An avid beachgoer in the 1950s and 1960s, Coleman recalled the time when he and a group of motorcycle- and automobile-racing enthusiasts left the beach in a cloud of dust, one group traveling south down the Buccaneer Trail while another group—including Coleman—chose the Youngblood Trail. Out from American Beach, Coleman's motorcade sped north and west up the county road. They cut through

Old Amelia Road, stirring up thick dust clouds. At the end of Old Amelia Road, deputies pulled out and gave chase. But the roadsters from Jacksonville knew that their cars could outrun the deputies'. At Highway A1A they headed northwest, traveling at a hundred miles an hour. Less than two minutes would see them off the island. Calvin Durham, who owned and drove a wide range of vehicles, led the motorcade, with Coleman a breath behind. When Youngblood's deputies realized they couldn't catch up with the speeding caravan, they called ahead for the bridge tender to raise the bridge. With the old drawbridge in sight, Durham sped up; he crossed the span while it was opening. Right behind him, Coleman went airborne, in the air for thirty feet, to land on the other side on all four tires. The car bounced and rocked but kept on going.[6] The others in the motorcade went to Cap'n Youngblood's jail.

CHAPTER 14

Law, Order, and Race

Would it please you if I strung my tears / In pearls for you to wear?
NAOMI MADGET

Any old-timer at American Beach will tell you the story of the Fourth of July, 1950, exactly as it is told here. I heard it from Charlotte Dwight Stewart, who was at the beach that year for the holiday with the rest of the Stewart clan.[1] At about four in the afternoon everyone's holiday festivities came to an abrupt end.

BLACK DEPUTIES IN NASSAU COUNTY

On that hot Fourth of July afternoon, a white deputy sheriff made insulting remarks to a black woman as he patrolled American Beach. He was riding in a car marked "H. J. Youngblood, Sheriff, Nassau County," and most people took him for the sheriff. Selma Richardson, who was there, said that "two Negroes, already drunk, reached through the window of the deputy's car and began cutting him. They nearly cut him to death."[2] As the deputy's intestines spilled out, a plea sounded across the beach thick with people. "Is there a doctor on the beach?" someone shouted through a bullhorn. "Is there a doctor on the beach? We need a doctor, please."

Dr. James Perry Patterson, president of the Jacksonville Medical and Dental and Pharmaceutical Association, responded. During those days of segregation and Jim Crow laws, no black doctor was allowed to treat a white person. But as the deputy lay near death, his fellow officers wanted any skilled physician. Before the deputy could safely be transported to a hospital, Patterson had to stitch his entrails in place. The doctor's neighbors later chastised him for answering the call, but for both Patterson and the deputy, this was one time race didn't matter.

Mildred Robinson Beltt, Jesse Patterson, and Allie Hart in front of the oceanfront home and office of Dr. and Mrs. James Patterson. Mrs. Patterson was renowned for her love of dogs and pigeons, both of which she trained. Courtesy Gwendolyn Leapheart.

Before sundown, every business had shut down, and crowds of people left the beach. While some deputies combed the dunes on American Beach to prevent the two assailants from escaping by car, other deputies raised the bridge over the Amelia River to block the island's only exit. Duck Davis recalls traffic coming to an absolute standstill as deputies thoroughly searched every car well into the night before letting people leave the island.[3] Sheriff Youngblood even deputized extra men to aid in the search, and many who remember the roadblock report that young white boys carrying rifles and shotguns were part of the posse that dark day.

But the men who slashed the deputy sheriff were never found. Some people believe they swam across Nassau Sound to Duval County. Some say they drowned.

The wounded deputy recovered, and not long afterward Sheriff Youngblood began looking for a black deputy, a Jackie Robinson type, to integrate the Nassau County Sheriff's Department. He found such a person in Jerry Maddox, who was recommended by the Business and Civic League, a respected organization in Fernandina's black business community. Maddox became the first black deputy in Nassau County since Reconstruction.

In 1954, while investigating a domestic disturbance, Maddox was shot and killed by a man he was attempting to arrest.[4] Tim Alberta, who was about ten at the time, heard the fatal shot and was there before Maddox's body was removed. Ten years later, Alberta was the first black officer hired by the City of Fernandina. Black deputies who followed Maddox in integrating the county sheriff's department were Curtis Telfair Sr. and Ben Sessions.

While the relationship between blacks and law enforcement officers has often been strained, assaults upon blacks at times have been inhumane almost beyond imagination. Such was the case when Chuck Smith was murdered by Nassau County deputies.

THE MURDER OF CHUCK SMITH

July 25, 1992, would turn out to be another dark day for American Beach law enforcement. It began at the Ocean Rendezvous, where a few locals sat around on that Saturday, teasing Chuck Smith about the chickens he kept. At thirty-eight, Chuck was a Vietnam vet who since the war had devoted his time to community service. He had helped rebuild homes for storm victims in St. Kitts and Nevis in the West Indies, volunteered at the St. Barnabas Center of the Episcopal Church, and gave his time and talent to

Chuck Smith (1954–1992) in 1980. A karate expert and Vietnam vet, Smith graduated from the University of San Francisco. Courtesy C. T. and Ruth Smith.

cooking at the Shrimp Festival for the American Beach, Inc. annual fundraiser. He also suffered mental and emotional problems as a result of combat. At the Rendezvous that day, he became angry at the teasing and reportedly threatened a man with a knife. Deputies were summoned to investigate.

Chuck's father, C. T. Smith, the local funeral director, said the deputies first talked to his son near the beach, where a sheriff's deputy whipped out his pistol and pointed it at his son's head while interviewing him. At this point, Chuck walked away from the four deputies into his home.

Extra deputies were requested to help those at the scene. With the additional backup, the deputies prepared to make an arrest, ordering the immediate neighborhood evacuated. Chuck was enlisted by his father to help carry his wheelchair-bound mother out of the house and did so in the presence of Sheriff Laurie Ellis's deputies. Mrs. Smith sat at the corner of the street with her husband and children, who had been summoned. Friends and neighbors were forbidden to speak with the family, who remained inside the police barricade, though a few like Marie Sessions and James Harris ignored the ropes and the deputies and stood vigil with the Smiths. For the next five hours, deputies and negotiators from the sheriff's office and mental health professionals tried to talk Chuck into leaving the house. When this failed, officers began to shoot into the home.

At 5:15 and continuing through the night, the police fired tear gas into the house. Chuck remained inside. As dusk set in, the deputies' volleys picked up, and by late in the evening the firing reached a frenzy. It seemed as though deputies were anxious to get their shots in. Toward midnight, Major Rocky Mistler was able to poke a hole through the wall into the bathroom where Chuck had taken refuge.

At that point, according to the Nassau County grand jury findings, "Mr. Smith was ordered to drop his weapon and surrender. When he did not, Lieutenant Hurst fired a shotgun through the hole and several deputies fired from the south and east sides of the house. Mr. Smith fell onto the bathroom floor and a team of deputies briefly entered the home to check his condition. It appeared at that time that Mr. Smith had been injured in the groin by the shotgun blast through the hole in the wall, but was still alive. The entry team was overcome by the tear gas in the house and hurriedly left. As they did, Mr. Smith allegedly attempted to raise his body. He was ordered to halt, but refused and was shot again by Lieutenant McDonald and Lieutenant Hurst from the south side of the house. These last shots were to the chest and head, and ultimately resulted in Mr. Smith's death."[5]

Chuck's father, C. T., tells a different story of the shot that killed his son. "The first shot that hit him went through his mouth and out from his head. He died instantly. The other shots to his body were after he was already dead."[6] Twenty bullets were found in Chuck Smith's body. There were also bullets in the beams of the house. The refrigerator looked like a target board. All the windows were shattered, and the stench of tear gas so permeated the house that it eventually had to be rebuilt.

The community was stunned. The next day when neighbors went through the barricaded area to return to their homes, police made casual joking remarks about the slaughter. One neighbor voiced the sentiment of the community in this letter to the editor of the *Fernandina News-Leader,* August 12, 1992:

He Raises Doubts about Vet's Death

I am a World War II veteran, having seen action in the Philippines, Okinawa, New Guinea, and the Solomon Islands. I was also a military policeman. After having worked for over 33 years for the Chrysler Corp. in Detroit, I retired with my family to live at American Beach. We loved the small town atmosphere and community closeness. Then on July 25, the "12 Hour Reign of Terror" happened and I am still in a state of shock! True, I have experienced all the combat pain of war, but the killing of Chuck Smith touched a deeper pain—one a father would feel for his son. Tears filled my eyes as questions circled my brain.

1. Why not simply wait it out? The lights and water were cut off. After all, he was in a windowless, small bathroom with no food.

2. Why didn't they use a tranquilizing gun? Where was the waiting helicopter if they really had intended to save him?

3. This black brother was a Navy Seal! If it had been a white vet at the [Amelia Island] Plantation, I am sure an experienced military psychiatrist would have been sent for from the Pentagon!

4. Why weren't some of his childhood sweethearts asked to speak to him? Love or fear are still the two strongest emotions.

5. Who gave the order to go in after him? If the police officers were tired, how strange they appeared the very next day with a business-as-usual attitude many residents found offensive. After all, they had just a few hours ago, just killed our neighbor!!

I did not know Chuck Smith personally. But I was there that night and a part of all of us died with him as we stood there helplessly questioning, "Is this Liberty and Justice for all?"

Harrison Perkins   American Beach

Less than two months later, Sheriff Ellis was defeated for re-election. The new sheriff relieved Lieutenant Larry MacDonald of his duties. On July 15, 1993, not quite a year after Chuck Smith died, Ellis was convicted in federal district court of seven drug-related charges and two obstruction of justice charges. On July 30 MacDonald was shot at close range following a robbery attempt on him in the parking lot of a Jacksonville store.[7] Both Ellis and Major Rocky Mistler, who had made many insensitive comments to Chuck Smith during the standoff and to the news media later, were convicted of selling confiscated drugs from the evidence room. On October 1 Ellis was sentenced to serve sixteen years in federal prison.[8] Mistler was sentenced to serve six years.[9]

CHAPTER 15

Driving on the Beach

Don't look back. Something might be gaining on you.
LEROY "SATCHEL" PAIGE

Driving on the beach was as much an American Beach tradition as build-ing sand castles, gathering seashells, or eating at Evans's Rendezvous. People drove the entire length of the thirteen-mile shoreline, as hard packed as a paved road, or watched the beach's Sunday drag races, or provided enter-tainment for onlookers as their own car wheels spun in the high-tide muck. Monday after Monday, all through the summer, drivers from Jacksonville and Georgia went to the Ford dealership on Eighth and Gum Streets in Fernandina to settle up their towing fees with Eugene Lasserre, the result of too much good timing and driving on the beach. And some years the ocean made off with a few cars.

ONE BIG TAILGATE PARTY

In the summers, as the tide receded, long rows of cars parked three deep on the half-mile beach, turning it into a super-size parking lot. Oceanfront tailgate parties lined the shore, dotting the sand with lounge chairs, beach umbrellas, ice chests, barbecue grills, and tables. From car trunks and truck beds, delicious foods and iced-down drinks were dispensed. As the tide began to roll back in, people inched their cars farther and farther back. Many left the beachfront altogether to stake out safer offshore parking space. Those who didn't heed the incoming tides paid a price. Often goodtimers who left their car on the beach while they went from one establishment to another found their vehicles floating in the ocean. Sometimes a car owner was right there when the tides rolled in but lingered a little too long before leaving.

Then the show began, with the driver (usually male) trying to be cool while his tires spun madly in the soft soupy sucking sands. Soon muscle-bodied guys with boards and shovels came to his aid, each dispensing instructions, solutions, and know-how as the tide continued to rise. Finally, the only thing to do was to call for the wrecker. The cars of those who waited too long would bob like floats in the ocean.

Every Sunday during the summer Eugene Lasserre of downtown Fernandina was called to tow cars out of the incoming tide. To be sure of getting his money, Lasserre lifted the front wheels of the distressed vehicle, jumped from the cab of his wrecker, and stuck his hand out for the five-dollar fee. If the driver didn't have the money, Lasserre said, "Put your spare tire on the back of the wrecker."[1] He used the spare as collateral.

Not everyone whose car suffered at the ocean's edge was guilty of neglect or hubris. Selma White Richardson was a professor of child psychology at Tuskegee Institute, and her husband, Dr. Harry V. Richardson, was the chaplain there. They traveled throughout the year the three hundred miles from Alabama to American Beach, the nearest with public lodging and accommodations for blacks. At first they stayed in one of the cabins the Afro reserved for their executives and other favored people, but eventually they built their own beach home.

During their first year at their beach cottage, the Richardsons drove one day to gather shells at the point at Nassau Sound, where then few walkers or motorists ventured. As they walked along the shore, a flash storm came up, and they were too far from their car to take shelter in it. Within a few minutes, the storm had passed, but not before filling their new 1941 Ford with sand, rain, and ocean water. As the tide rapidly rose around the car, its horn bleated sorrowfully. The Richardsons walked home in disbelief.[2]

Harry and Selma Richardson and their 1953 Ford in front of their cottage on the hill, winter 1954. Harry Richardson was founder and president of the Atlanta University Seminary. During the summer beach season, the Richardsons attended weekly Sunday school lessons at A. L. Lewis's home. Courtesy Selma Richardson.

Drag Racing

Horse-drawn carriages had raced on Amelia Beach as far back as 1880, and car races were common events during the 1920s. From the 1950s to the early 1970s unsanctioned drag races took place almost one mile south of Evans's Rendezvous, right at the beachfront of Amelia Island Plantation.

In Jacksonville, Ben Darby and his best friend, Earl Harris, would gather their running buddies, Freddie and Daryle Richardson, Gilbert and Sandra Jones Gadson, Gene Belton, and a few others on Saturdays to make detailed plans for a super Sunday on the salt. They tinkered with their cars, shopped for slabs of spareribs to barbecue, and called around the riverfront fish markets to see which had the biggest live crabs at fifty cents a dozen. Saturday nights they played bid whist and other card games. Since no alcohol was sold in Duval County on Sunday, they bought beer for the next day before the bars in Jacksonville closed at midnight.[3]

Sunday afternoons found Ben's caravan on the beach cheering Gilbert Gadson in his fire-engine red 1963d-1/2 Ford Galaxy 5 fastback, a beauty of a model that came on the market between the 1963 and 1964 Galaxies. Gadson's, with a 390-cubic-inch engine, a four-barrel carburetor, a red interior, and bucket seats, looked like a winner, but only Sandra, Gilbert's wife, never Gilbert himself, could take it to victory lane. Finally, Gilbert gave in and worked on the car and Sandy did the racing.

After talking with John J. Coleman, who entered the weekly races on the beach from 1957 to 1963, it's easy to see why Gilbert's car had such a hard time winning. Coleman, the mentor of many students and driver education teacher at Stanton High School in Jacksonville in the 1950s, entered his 1963 Ford Galaxy 500 in the Sunday races on the salt. Cars were his passion. A crackerjack mechanic, he souped up his car during the week at his service station and mechanic shop, where he modified cars for the races he entered throughout the region. Through the years, Coleman had raced a Lincoln, a Chevrolet, and a Buick, but his best racing car was his last, the Galaxy 500. It may have looked just like Gilbert Gadson's, but under the hood were two four-barrel carburetors and a 427-cubic-inch engine with 425 horsepower. Coleman won races on the beach every Sunday he raced there.[4]

Auto racers made bets on their cars, one driver against another, from fifty to a hundred dollars per race. To keep down disputes and prevent reneging on bets at the end of the race, Deputy Sheriff Curtis Telfair held the money

Race-car driver John J. Coleman, 1963. Coleman changed the oil in his cars every other day and tore up many rear ends during the six years he raced on American Beach and other Florida tracks. Courtesy Mary Coleman.

that each driver put up before taking off. Coleman tricked drivers into betting against him through a ruse that involved Gilbert Gadson's car. Gilbert's 63 1/2 ran first, winning some and losing some; he and his cronies struggled until they'd had enough and left. After Gilbert's car limped away from the arena, Coleman cruised on in. When boys from Georgia and others who didn't know him spotted Coleman, they thought it was the same car that had been beaten earlier, and they eagerly took up the bet against Coleman and his pit crew. By now the sidelines would be solid people. Coleman's car could reach a speed of 175 on the quarter-mile strip, after which he and his crew gathered up their winnings.

Coleman's racing days ended in 1963 in Jacksonville. About ten o'clock one November night on his way home from the shop, Coleman was flying low down Edgewood Avenue; his speedometer read eighty, and he was still in second gear. When the driver in a car ahead signaled a left turn and Coleman swung to the right to pass, the driver turned right instead, into her driveway. Coleman tore up her car's rear end, and her car tore down her carport. Coleman's car spun around in the air, crossed the ditch, and plowed up her yard. After paying for the damages, repairing his car, and looking death so close in the face, Coleman knew that it was time for him to make a change. He sold the car and devoted himself to the auto mechanic shop, where he still tinkers with cars today.

Races on the beach continued, even after Sheriff Youngblood retired. The new sheriff's officers didn't get involved with car-racing politics, however; when they went to the race strip, it was to quell the fire. With drag-racing participants running their own affairs, disputes often flared up about who crossed the finish line first. Lieutenant Tim Alberta recalls being on the scene one Sunday some years back, when several arrests had to be made. Before the paddy wagon had driven three blocks up Lewis Street on the way to the jail, they received a call for back-up enforcement on the beach because shooting had begun.[5] More paddy wagons were called out to bring peace among car-racing friends.

High Flying

Many children and parents took their first airplane rides from the shoreline of American Beach. On Saturdays and Sundays adventurous beachgoers lined up to wait their turn for a seat on the single-engine plane that would carry them around Nassau Sound, over to the Amelia River, and back down on the beach to pick up the next group of four passengers ready to part with two dollars apiece. The only sights they saw were the ocean, trees, and streams, as there was no development on the southern end of the island, aside from American Beach, the twelve families of Franklin Town, and the few inhabitants of Amelia City. But taking a ride provided boasting status; you could then say that you had flown in an airplane.

Chip Oxley, whose family owned the funeral home in downtown Fernandina, was the pilot. Tim Alberta remembers his first and last ride with Oxley. The takeoff was uneventful, but once they were high enough, Oxley cut the engine, and they dropped from the sky until Oxley thought it was time to get the engine restarted. Then they glided in for a smooth landing off shore. That trick did it for Tim. Boasting rights or no, he decided that he'd had one ride too many.

When the Amelia Island Company developed Amelia Island Plantation, the organization found a law on the books that prohibited the racing of cars on the beach and persuaded the county to enforce it—for if the county wouldn't, the state would. That was the final checkered flag for car racing on the salt.

~~~~~~~~~~ CHAPTER 16

Stewartville at A1A

A sure way for one to lift himself up is by helping to lift someone else.
BOOKER T. WASHINGTON

In Amelia City, up the road from American Beach, is an area the locals call Stewartville, because a goodly number of the Stewart clan live there. Besides the community's close geographic connection with American Beach, the Stewart family has proven helpful and resourceful to beach residents for well over half a century, so that a spirit of kinship exists between these two neighbors.

MUTUAL BENEFITS

A. L. Lewis called on the Stewarts to fell gigantic trees and uproot ancient forest growth, preparing the land at American Beach for home sites and vehicular access. With the aid of horses and wagons and a mule named Ned, Hayes Stewart and his sons leveled virgin woods and uninhabitable dunes into building pads and roads. Dunes were seen as something that blocked the view rather than as a buffer against shoreline erosion.

For clearing the land Stewart earned seven dollars a week, plus an additional sum for each dune that he leveled. His young sons, Willie and Alexander, worked with him and received twenty-five cents a day, a generous sum for a teen and preteenager during the middle of the Depression. At the end of the week, of the $1.50 in the Stewart boys' pay envelope, they had to donate twenty-five cents to Lewis's church, Mt. Olive AME.[1] Actually, anybody Lewis employed was asked to make weekly donations to the church. The Stewart boys shelled out again when they got home; there were fourteen siblings. When it was all settled, Willie and his younger brother Alex each had a nickel to spend for themselves at the end of a six-day work week.

When roads were surveyed and ready to be paved, the Stewarts loaded mounds of oyster shells onto trucks, shovel by shovel, and by the shovelful they emptied the shells from the trucks into the roadbeds. A few years older now, they earned twenty-five cents an hour.

Lewis wanted to pay off his indebtedness to the family and offered to send two of Stewart's sons, Leonard and Willie, to Stanton High School in Jacksonville and then on for further studies at Bethune-Cookman College. Hayes and his wife, Josephine Hopkins Stewart, encouraged their sons all through the summer to take advantage of this educational opportunity; they must go to Jacksonville, live with the Lewis family, go to school. The boys, however, were afraid of leaving their family and wanted to stay at home. When the final day came, only Leonard got into the rumble seat of Lewis's chauffeur-driven green Buick, and he wasn't gone a day before Lewis's chauffeur, Ollie, brought him back home. The Stewarts wanted an education, but they weren't willing to leave the island to get it. Willie admired Lewis, but living in his house meant living under the thumb of Lewis's wife, Elzona. The Stewarts opted for their freedom on Amelia Island.

SHEILA SHEPHERD

Sixty years later, an opportunity for a descendant of the Stewart family to go to college came to Sheila Shepherd, the epitome of a youth role model. Through scholastic achievement, service, and merit, Sheila became the recipient of several college scholarships. When she graduated from Fernandina Beach High School in 1993, scholarships for her continuing education were there. They came from business and civic organizations throughout the island community, I. T. T. Rayonier Paper Mill, Amelia Island Golf Association, Women's Club of Fernandina, Fernandina Friends of the Library, Nassau County Volunteer Association, American Business Women Association, University Scholars, and others from colleges and universities. This

Willie C. and Bonnie Matthews of Stewartville at a Labor Day American Beach Taste Fest. In the 1950s, Bonnie's aunt, L'Questra Everett, bought Stewartville from its original owner, Everett Means, and named the streets in honor of her grandchildren. Courtesy Michael Phelts.

was one of Stewartville's proudest moments, and a glorious feeling for American Beach as well. Sheila accepted the challenge and enrolled in the School of Nursing at the University of North Florida in Jacksonville with these scholarships.

This was a bittersweet time, for Sheila's, mother, Elizabeth, died in early spring 1993, just before Sheila's graduation, but she had to know that her daughter would do just fine. Sheila's accomplishments have made the Stewarts and the communities of this island proud.[21]

The Honey Dripper

Stewartville's official name is Everett Acres, named for Everett Means, nephew of Gabriel Means.[2] Shortly after active duty in World War II, Everett Means returned to the island and in 1946 invested his savings and bonuses in land a few miles north of Franklin Town. His property began at Highway A1A, then ran eastward toward the ocean. Means and his wife, Juanita, built a home there, and in the 1950s, a first-class bar and restaurant, the Honey Dripper. Half a mile from American Beach, the establishment's name beamed out in neon lights in front of the yellow brick structure with plate-glass picture windows. It wasn't long before word got around that this was the place to be. The Honey Dripper's regular clientele hung out until the wee hours of the morning. This was the late night stop-off place for gay poppers who didn't want to quit after Evans's Rendezvous had closed and the beach began to wind down.

FREDERICK'S SCENIC VIEW RESTAURANT

Across the street from the Honey Dripper was Frederick's Scenic View Restaurant, a serene retreat from the bustle on American Beach. Reddie and Alfreda Frederick built this eatery on a marsh along the Amelia River. Their restaurant had a light, airy, and sparkling clean atmosphere. The proprietors took time to chat with diners as their seafood dinners were being prepared. Guests placed orders and browsed in the gift shop while awaiting their meals, the best-prepared food on the island. The Fredericks brought

Shelia Shepherd (third from left) accepting a scholarship for the study of anesthesiology from the Fernandina Men's Golf Association. With Shelia are Cyndi Roberts, association president Frank Finocchio, Carl Bouin, and Jody Jones. Courtesy *Fernandina Beach News-Leader.*

souvenirs from Miami, where they lived and worked from November through April.

Outside diners watched the sun setting on the Amelia River. In early evening, flocks of egrets, herons, gulls, and other shore birds flew to nearby trees to roost. Songbirds in adjacent woods serenaded the diners. On some evenings, the crickets and cicadas emitted a racket-making clicking that overpowered any other sounds. Their concert might go on for twenty minutes, then fall silent until the next evening. Other times a frog chorus bellowed wild rounds of croaking. All of this made for an enjoyable feast of sights and sounds for diners on the marsh side of the island.

This restaurant catered to discerning diners and drew its customers, including white patrons, from many communities throughout the island as well as tourists. American Beach visitors favored this retreat on weekends and summer holidays, but Alfreda Frederick could recall weeks of workdays when she wouldn't see a black person in the restaurant other than her husband.[4]

For twenty-five years, the restaurant operated from April to November. Right after they closed for the season in November 1979, Reddie Frederick became ill. They didn't return to Miami that year, and he died the following April. Their charming restaurant never reopened for business. For the next eight years, Alfreda Frederick lived in their home on the marsh. When she knew that she would not open the business again, she sold it. She was an islander, born on the northernmost end of Fernandina in Old Town. Her siblings encouraged her to move into town, closer to all of the family, and she agreed to do so. The restaurant was demolished in 1991. In the circular drive of Frederick's Scenic View Restaurant, a cabbage palm and a juniper tree are all that remain.

The Irony of Civil Rights

At the banquet table of nature there are no reserved seats. You get what you can take, and you keep what you can hold. If you can't take anything, you won't get anything; and if you can't hold anything you won't keep anything. And you can't take anything without organization.

A. PHILIP RANDOLPH

The American Beach that grew and prospered under segregation all but vanished with the passage of the Civil Rights Act, July 2, 1964. In the 1970s and 1980s, A. L. Lewis's grandchildren and great-grandchildren sold their beach homes and property.[1]

The parking lot was sold, and the A. L. Lewis Motel.[2] The run-down rental cabins were demolished. Just as the beach had been bought by the parcel during the 1930s and 1940s, so was it sold. The last parcel, nearly a hundred acres, was sold in the declining years of the Afro-American Life Insurance Company, which had become the New Century Corporation.[3] The new owners of this tract of the original Samuel Harrison Grant, Anthony J. Leggio, Ronald J. Nemeyer, and Dominic J. Blondi, paid $790,000 for it. Shortly after that exchange, neither the Afro nor any member of the Lewis family owned a home or property on American Beach.

A beach cottage, now abandoned to time and neglect. Courtesy Michael Phelts.

At first the decline of the beach was blamed on Hurricane Dora's aftermath. But when several businesses were rebuilt and new establishments opened, and the big beach crowds still did not show up, people came to realize that the decline was largely the result of black flight.

The civil rights legislated in 1964 had opened all public facilities to African Americans. Former American Beach vacationers and day-trippers now frolicked on Miami Beach, raced up and down the wide sands at Daytona, wore out the cobblestones of Savannah, and rode high at St. Simons Island. All along the shores of the East Coast, blacks explored areas that had once been off limits. The three-day weekends at American Beach shrank to one day; the Sunday visitors and day-trippers no longer stayed overnight. Loaded buses no longer caused a bottleneck at the crossroads. With so little business most of the restaurants and resort establishments closed.

The Amelia Island Company

In 1970, the Amelia Island Company began to buy up property on the southern end of the island.[4] The plan was to develop from the eastern shores of Amelia City to American Beach, Franklin Town, and on to where Nassau Sound joined the Amelia River. They came intending to buy half of the mostly undeveloped shoreline on Amelia Island.

The Amelia Island Company successfully acquired the property at Frank-lintown.[5] It purchased a huge chunk of land for a warehouse and mainte-nance plant just inside the American Beach entrance and also bought the property northeast of American Beach that Summer Beach owns today.[6] The company waited to buy up American Beach, anticipating that prop-erty owners would eventually be eager to sell.

Meanwhile, however, employees of the Amelia Island Company sought to buy their own property on American Beach. They found ready sellers, and several oceanfront and ocean-view homes were sold in a sweep by aging owners. Older homes began to show deterioration and neglect. A third of the small oceanfront was sold to buyers who were not African Americans.

But the Amelia Island Company and their employees overbought, and the company declared bankruptcy. Those on American Beach who had sold their properties got them back because the terms and conditions of the mortgage deeds were not fulfilled. Yet for a variety of reasons, many were still ready to divest themselves of their property, and it was at this point that American Beach baby boomers from around the country returned to the beach they had visited with their parents thirty or forty years earlier. They came back as buyers of property and builders of homes.

Baby Boomers' S.O.S.

One such investor in the 1980s was Jack James Jr., who bought and hand-somely restored the first house on American Beach, originally built for A. L. Lewis. James, an entrepreneur and building contractor, bought many other beach properties as well.

Ruth Waters-McKay also scooped up several unwanted beach properties during the selling frenzy. For many years, she successfully encouraged black families to "buy the property now, and build your dream house later."

Eugene Emory of Philadelphia, who juked in the juke joints on American Beach in the 1960s while a student at Edward Waters College, returned twenty years later as Dr. Emory, a clinical researcher at Emory University Hospital in Atlanta. He found much of the oceanfront deserted, with "For sale" signs on many home sites. He bought several pieces of vacated ocean-front properties and aesthetically rearranged the architectural design of the one he lives in from a plain saltbox facade to a gingerbread trim. Through-out the community, many others did the same.

A number of community members fought to curb black flight. Frank and

A 1992 photo of American Beach's first house, originally built in 1935 for A. L. Lewis, renovated by Jacksonville builder and owner Jack James. Courtesy Michael Phelts.

Above: Owen and Ruth Waters-McKay attending the Bausch and Lomb women's tennis tournament at Amelia Island Plantation, 1991. Courtesy Michael Phelts.

Right: Ruth Waters-McKay in the office of Connie Mack, then U.S. senator from Florida. Waters-McKay led a delegation to Washington, D.C., seeking congressional support for the development of municipal services on American Beach. Courtesy Michael Phelts.

Johnell Preliou (left), president of the Fernandina Nassau County NAACP, and Eugene Emory at the dedication of Burney Park on American Beach, October 20, 1990. Courtesy James Robinson.

Emma Morgan, who owned an oceanfront home, pleaded with landowners not to sell, to hold on to their properties and maintain this unique African American coastal resort. But other property owners sold lot after lot and home after home. As the selling frenzy continued, the Morgans bought vacant lots along the ocean by the dozen.

Another property owner, Ben Durham Jr., and his family also believed in the beach's future. On oceanfront property Durham bought from the Afro, he built a one-room efficiency unit to serve as family headquarters. Durham

The first Durham family home was the little shed in the right background, where the Durhams sheltered from the weather on beach trips. Later the four-unit apartment in the foreground became a vacation home, owned today by John and Willie Mae Hayes of Atlanta and Jacksonville. Courtesy Michael Phelts.

Ben Durham, then principal of Stanton High School in Jacksonville, built this home for his sister and brother-in-law, Dorothy and William Lucas. Courtesy Michael Phelts.

and his siblings all had families as well as many friends stopping by to visit, and in time the one room grew into a two-story, three-unit condominium where family and friends wore out the view weekend after weekend. Even with black flight in high gear, Durham's siblings bought up available ocean-front properties, on which Durham built them beautiful vacation homes.

AMERICAN BEACH, INC.

Ben Durham founded American Beach, Inc., for the perpetuation and preservation of the coastal community he loved. The group's charter, issued on February 26, 1982, by the State of Florida, has been in continuous opera-

Ben Durham Jr., shown here in 1980, chartered American Beach, Inc., in February 1982 and served as its president until his death in 1986. Courtesy Dot Durham Lucas.

tion since. The initial board of directors were Ben Durham Jr., president; Myrtis C. Thomas, secretary; Dr. Elizabeth Jones (Boddie), Maxcell Wilson, Mrs. I. E. (Mamma) Williams, and Leroy Tyler. Upon Durham's death in 1986, Frank Morgan Sr. became president. Presidents who followed Morgan were Bobby Dollison, Circuit Court judge Henry Lee Adams Jr., and Annette McCollough Myers.

American Beach, Inc., meets in the Fellowship Hall of the Franklin Town United Methodist Church, a historic building that was moved to American Beach from its original Franklin Town location. Among the community improvements owed to this group are a quarter-mile continuous sidewalk from AIA to Ocean Boulevard and a two-acre tract designated for a community center. Through a beautification project on Lewis street, 150 palms, live oaks, and holly trees now enhance the quarter-mile leading to the ocean.

People like Ben Durham and the founding officers and board of directors of American Beach, Inc., showed great foresight when they decided to buy up property at American Beach and to encourage those there to remain. However, while individuals bought lots, the developers bought parcels. This was a beach for sale.

American Beach, Inc., sponsored the organizing of the American Beach 4-H Club. Here Torrie Gilyard fills out an application to become a 4-H charter member in 1992, as American Beach, Inc., president Annette Myers looks on. Courtesy Michael Phelts.

CHAPTER 18

The Beach Rejuvenated

Let a new earth rise, let another world be born. Let a bloody peace be written in the sky. Let a second generation full of courage issue forth; let a people loving freedom come to growth.
MARGARET WALKER

Owning a home or property on American Beach was never limited to the well-to-do. In the beginning, oceanfront lots sold for $200. Today vacant oceanfront lots range from $85,000 to more than $100,000. On the west end, referred to as "the no-water end," lots have always been cheaper and today range from $15,000 to $45,000. Asking prices for existing homes on the "no-water end" start at $60,000. While the opulent buildings of our neighbors to the south on Amelia Island Plantation, to the north at Summer Beach/Ritz Carlton, or to the west at Plantation Point/Florence Point are not to be found on American Beach, the community boasts a number of fine homes. Many people seeking to buy property on American Beach arrive hoping to buy a lean-to or a shanty; something they can fix up themselves, but if it's a lean-to on the ocean, the going price is $200,000.

Left: The boathouse home of John Telfair Holmes, 1992. Courtesy Michael Phelts.

Middle: The home of Frances and George Green, 1992. George Green is the principal caretaker of the Franklin Town Cemetery, where hundreds of his ancestors are buried. Homes in the Plantation Point Development have been built over the graves, threatening the cemetery, once a two-acre plot, with destruction. Courtesy Michael Phelts.

A 1994 view of Summer Beach, the resort that adjoins American Beach to the north. Courtesy Gary McElwee.

The Ocean Boulevard hilltop home designed and built by
William Watson in 1989. Courtesy Michael Phelts.

The former Broadnax home, which became the home of Ben
and Marie Sessions in 1975. The Sessions added the second
floor. Courtesy Michael Phelts.

Beach Business Today

During the community's golden era, businesses proliferated—Evans's Rendezvous, Williams Guest Lodge, El Patio, Reynolds's Sandwich Shop, Logan's Barbecue, Little Zeng's Restaurant and Ice Cream Shop, Simmons's Restaurant, Sweet Tooth Ice Cream and Candy Shop, Tino's Restaurant, Williams Quick Snack, Cowart's Motel and Restaurant. A half-mile off the beach in Stewartville, people could frequent Frederick's Scenic View Restaurant and the Honey Dripper Restaurant and Lounge.

Today, as in American Beach's developing years, only one beach-season business remains, apart from lodging facilities—the Ocean Rendezvous, open some Saturdays and all Sundays. The community's founding father, A. L. Lewis, did not intend that there be public business establishments there. Lewis envisioned a resort community of private homes and lodging facilities that the Afro would provide for executives and influential clients.

Beachgoers also keep an eye out for the erratic openings of Net's Place and Little Zeng. Jeanette Mobley, who owns these businesses, opens them for the use of her very large and extended family. But the American Beach community makes itself welcome and at home. The niece of Alfreda Frederick, the former proprietor of Frederick's Scenic View Restaurant, Mobley makes crab cakes from her aunt's recipe, using 100 percent blue crabmeat. Her creole vegetable medley comes fresh from her father's garden in Yulee, ten miles west of Amelia Island.

Besides the approximately one hundred single-family homes in the community, there is one oceanfront motel, American Beach Villas, the former A. L. Lewis Motel. Since the early 1980s, Bobby Dollison of Atlanta and Diane Desmond have owned and operated the Villas year-round. Other

Little Zeng and Net's Place, a family vacation home and diner for the Mobleys of Yulee, Florida, 1992. Courtesy Michael Phelts.

oceanfront lodgings available for vacationers include a posh, five-unit contemporary condominium, whose third-floor penthouse offers a view from the southern point of the island to the northernmost. Eugene Emory of Atlanta is the principal owner of this oceanfront complex. The new owners of the former Durham place are John and Willie May Hayes of Atlanta and Jacksonville; who have developed it into modern resort units. Several family homes also offer guest lodging.

First Family Descendants

Through the years, American Beach has been the permanent residence of approximately thirty families. Five of these families—the Greens, Jeffersons, Thomases, Wilsons, and Drummonds—trace their heritage on the island to before the Civil War.

Above: Larry Goodwin and his golden lab, Odie, joined the American Beach community for Cleanup Day on March 28, 1992. Courtesy Michael Phelts.

Right: Jimmy Drummond (1826–1933), ca. 1920. A veteran of the Civil War, Drummond came to Amelia Island with a small band of Indians from the Everglades in about 1846 and settled on the old Harrison plantation at the island's south end. Courtesy Eartha White Collection, University of North Florida, Jacksonville.

Marvyne Betsch in 1993. Marvyne, popularly known as "the Beach Lady," is a seventh-generation descendant of Zephaniah and Anna Kingsley and the great-granddaughter of A. L. Lewis. Courtesy Ivy Bigbee.

Eccentric is the word most often used to describe the great-granddaughter of A. L. Lewis, Marvyne Betsch, "Beach Lady." The first child of Mary Lewis and John Betsch, she returned to the beach in 1977 and has since then camped and homesteaded on the property of several absentee homeowners along the oceanfront. The same word was used to describe another of her ancestors, Zephaniah Kingsley. Lydia Maria Child, who interviewed Kingsley in 1842, described him as short but appearing much larger upon his great white stallion and in the large sombrero he almost always wore, along with a poncho and silver-buckled shoes with thick heels.[1]

Seven generations later Marvyne Betsch wraps herself in a self-styled poncho 365 days a year, topped with a black lace veil she wears like a headband. She alters the spelling and pronunciation of her name frequently to suit her moods or causes. She is tall, as was her ancestor Anna Kingsley, and like her knows the value of trees. According to legend, Anna Kingsley supervised the planting of 143 palmetto palms along Palmetto Avenue, the road to Kingsley Plantation on Fort George Island. Approximately 150 years later, Marvyne was a part of the tree-planting project on American Beach that put in nearly 150 trees on Lewis Street, helping water the trees near the ocean until they took root.

Marvyne graduated high in her class from Oberlin Conservatory of Music and went on to sing *Madame Butterfly* and *Carmen* in Germany. Her sister, Johnnetta Betsch Cole, an anthropologist and author, became the first African American woman president of Spelman College in Atlanta. Her brother, John Betsch, an internationally acclaimed percussionist, lives in Paris.

Ernestine Latson Smith and her family live in the home built by her maternal grandfather, Louis Dargan Ervin, the Afro's general manager when American Beach was founded.

Many beach home and property owners and visitors are from Alabama. When long-time property owners on American Beach are asked today about the Alabama connection, they credit Afro executive Ralph Stewart Sr. with having promoted the beach to the Tuskegee professors and physicians from the veterans' hospital there. Stewart's grandson, Michael Stewart, and his

Ernestine Latson Smith, granddaughter of Afro-American Life Insurance Company founder E. W. Latson and agent-secretary Louis Dargan Ervin, 1993. Courtesy James Robinson.

family live in the duneside home constructed in the early days of American Beach development by his grandparents, Ralph and Marie Stewart.

If history repeats itself, American Beach may be good for another half century. Before its development, the original African American community of Franklin Town lasted more than a century on Amelia Island; American Beach has been there only sixty years.

American Beach community leader Michael Stewart, 1988. In 1995 Stewart was appointed to the Jacksonville Transportation Authority by Florida governor Lawton Chiles. Courtesy Michael Stewart.

From Winter Shelling to Virgo Bash

Where does one run when he's already in the promised land?
CLAUDE BROWN

Any day on American Beach is a day of beauty, no matter the weather or season. From solitary shelling in winter to the exuberant crowds of September's Virgo Bash, the variety of activities and moods run a delightful gamut.

WINTER

While fishing on American Beach is excellent, collecting and gathering seashells is even more popular. In the still of winter, a blanket of large shells covers the shore—whole heart-shaped cockle shells, ten-inch pen shells, olives, moon shells. James and Jeanie Harris, the biggest shell collectors on the beach, load their jeep with these and a variety of conchs, cockles, angel wings, scallops, nutmegs, tulips, and on and on. From their plentiful collection James Harris creates sea critters for American Beach, Inc.'s exhibits and tours.

When Gwen Leapheart and her entourage go shelling, you might imagine that an armored truck had dropped silver dollars all over the beach, judging by the serious and intense manner in which the shellers comb the shore. Larry and Charlotte Burwell, who gather shells from American Beach during the winter and from Martha's Vineyard during the summer, share a beach home with Leapheart. They incorporate shells in the beautiful lamps, pictures, and candles that they give away for the asking all over the beach.

Winter brings hundreds of pelicans and seagulls to the shore, unintimidated by joggers or walkers. Between nine o'clock and noon, gulls, ospreys, and hawks fly across highway A1A, from American Beach south to Talbot Island, fish in their talons, headed for a roost in a tree or on a telephone pole to enjoy their fresh catch. The seagulls partake of shelling as well as fishing. On shell-picking days, they carry four-inch cockle shells up a distance, drop the shells to crash on the hard sand, then dive in for a repast of succulent clams.

In Calhoun Park, a block-long private park and garden owned by John and Frances Calhoun, flowers bloom among the trees and foliage twelve months of the year. The Calhouns' primary home is in O'Neal, the first community west of Amelia Island.

So inviting and appealing is their park that for years passersby pulled in and set up for the day, using the Calhouns' water, electricity, benches, tables,

Best friends since the days of their childhood romps on American Beach, St. Frances Darby Daniels, Mike Phelts, and James Daniels enjoy a day of fellowship at the Phelts beach playhouse in 1992. Courtesy Michael Phelts.

The road to American Beach has been long traveled year-round. Nettye Leapheart entertained friends from New York during winter months. Here is Nettye,
on the left, with Pansy McPhaden Hicks, Allie Hart, and Mildred Robinson
Beltt, ca. 1950. Courtesy Gwendolyn Leapheart.

and grills. The Calhouns eventually fenced in the area and entertained their
families and guests there when they were on the beach.[1]

Surrounding the community, dense woods of century-old trees are still
filled with wild creatures. Opossums and raccoons all but walk up and lay
themselves down on grills or in ovens. What often begins as a garden stroll
for a gopher or turtle often ends in a simmering stewpot by way of an old-
time resident and the kitchen chopping block. The same fate awaits small
game that don't make it from one side of the road to the other, especially in
the winter. American Beach folk make no apologies for cooking and serving the indigenous game they have long enjoyed.

Spring and Summer

In the breezy days of spring, leaves on the oak and magnolia trees look as
though they had been dipped in apple green paint and polished. The sound
of trucks and jeeps barreling down Lewis Street more often notifies the community that the season is changing, that the busiest time of year is approach-

ing. Those who maintain vacation cottages visit more frequently, and family and friends who know you are on the beach make impromptu house calls. The Sunday attendance and number of cars at the Franklin Town United Methodist Church increase.

In summer, many households host guests who have come to enjoy American Beach–style picnics, crab boils, or fish fries. As early as four in the morning, songbirds tune up. As the day warms up, all along Lewis Street residents watch from porches and swings as group after group of visitors heads for the ocean. As evening shadows increase, fireflies light up the night and the moon shines silver on the sea. Some evenings birdsong lasts into the night and through early morning. Birdwatchers may be rewarded with the sight of pileated woodpeckers teaching their young the tricks of foraging through trees.

The healthy woods have made American Beach a bird sanctuary. More than two hundred species have been observed on the island since 1990, a record regarded as a status symbol throughout the community.[2] Cardinals perform daily evening recitals; colonies of pileated woodpeckers frequently visit yards and are as common as blue jays. Energetic fish crows keep the area free of discarded picnic food. House sparrows build nests in idle mailboxes and in the eaves of houses. An abundance of mockingbirds, wrens, and robins sound blissful melodies.

A fishing party visiting American Beach from Camden County, Georgia, in 1993. Courtesy Michael Phelts.

Cutting the ribbon at the Burney Park dedication at American Beach, October 24, 1990. Left to right: Marsha Dean Phelts, Mrs. I. H. Burney, and Nassau County commissioner Jim B. Higginbotham. Courtesy *Fernandina Beach News-Leader*.

The public park at American Beach, the Burney Road Beach Front Park, completed and dedicated in the fall of 1990, sees most of its customers in the summer. This six-acre county park came about through an agreement between the Nassau County Commissioners, the Amelia Island Company, and Plantation Park. To ensure adequate entrances to the beaches, the county negotiated with developers to dedicate some land for public access. Thus when Tony Leggio of Plantation Park purchased the last parcel of land from the Afro, eighty-four acres, the county encouraged him to contribute a portion for a park at the southeast end of Burney Road. The park adjoins the property of Amelia Island Plantation, which contributed five acres, including two hundred feet of ocean frontage valued at $740,000. The Plantation's homeowners' association granted the park an easement for water hookup, as well as $150,000 toward development of this park.[3] The county constructed an oceanfront park with a bath and shower house, restrooms, drinking fountains, as well as an outside shower stall, covered picnic pavilions, and two hundred parking spaces, with eleven designated for buses or recreation vehicles. A basketball court should soon be added. The park and all facilities are free and open to the public year round.

Burney Park was named in honor of Isadore Horace Burney II of Athens, Georgia, who began a long association with the Afro-American Life Insurance Company when he served as an agent in Athens and later as district manager in Savannah, Tampa, and Atlanta. In 1954 he moved to Jacksonville to become secretary of the company. He served as president from 1967 until 1975 and was also president of the National Insurance Association for the 1972–73 term. Burney and his bride, Miriam Cunningham of Atlanta, visited the beach briefly in 1936, and from that time on, he and his family regularly vacationed there.[4] In 1965, he built a home there, which is still enjoyed by his family.

During the final days of summer there are deep purple scuppernongs, or wild grapes, for the picking everywhere. The sidewalk all down Lewis Street is stained from the deep purple juices that splatter from overripe unpicked grapes hanging in branches overhead. All through the woods, grapes and blackberries beckon. Many residents make a year's supply of jelly from the grapes, known locally as opossum grapes, since they're also popular with those nocturnal animals. These plentiful grapes grow wild on the mangroves of the island and in field patches, clinging to fences or hanging from four-inch-thick vines that wind around towering trees. Bay trees too cover the island. A cook may snap a cluster of bay leaves from outside the door and drop them in a cooking pot or onto a smoking grill to spice up a meal.

AUTUMN—AND VIRGO BASH

Many organizations and auxiliary church groups plan activities on American Beach in the warm, sunny days of fall. The general pace is more leisurely, the wildflowers throughout the community more brilliant, the squirrels busier harvesting acorns and walnuts. After shucking the seeds from pinecones, the squirrels command attention by dropping hard pine cones and stripped shavings at those walking near the trees. A mockingbird may chase a squirrel and whip it up and down a tree trunk for playing too close to the bird's nest.

The biggest and most fish I've seen caught from surf fishing have always been in the fall. If you happen along the shore while a commercial or sports crew is out seining, and you have something to put the throwbacks in, you can come away with large bluefish, catfish, whiting, pompanos, drums, crabs, conchs—almost anything but big flounder and red bass. These get paraded up and down the shore before being rushed home for family dinner.

Some people assume that the beach closes after Labor Day; they pack up, go home, and are not seen until the next spring—and they miss the biggest party on American Beach, the annual Virgo Bash. Originated by Michael and Lydia Stewart and Brenda Onfroy on September 15, 1985, to celebrate

Royal Family members arriving at the 1988 Virgo Bash. Left to right: Sam Daniels, Byer Webb, Debra Giddens, Valerie Clark, Michael Stewart, Rudy Quarles, Lydia Stewart, and Lauretta Hansberry-Mimms. Courtesy Michael Stewart.

Mike's birthday, the bash began as a one-day affair. The next year, while compiling a list of close friends, the trio realized that many of their invitees shared the same birth month, and they decided to share the celebration. Virgo Bash was born and shortly spread over the entire weekend.

The Stewarts and Onfroy organized a Virgo Club, whose members were known as the Royal Family. Each year they wear specially ordered t-shirts,

Master chef Dennis Stewart and fellow Royal Family members Brenda Onfroy and Thea Richardson preparing important ingredients for a Virgo Bash feast, 1990. Courtesy Michael Stewart.

Succulent appetizers launch the first course of a Virgo Bash feast. Clockwise from front left: Rudy Quarles, Sharon Gordon, Linda Stewart (at the head of the table), Tina Smith, Debra Giddens, and Byer Webb. Courtesy Michael Stewart.

Circuit Court judge Brian Davis at the 1993 Virgo Bash picking succulent morsels of blue crab while waiting for the beach whitings to fry. Courtesy Michael Phelts.

and each year the party attracts more friends from across the country. They come from California, New York, Texas, Atlanta, Washington, D.C., Virginia, Maryland, and all over the state of Florida. One year a guest traveled to Virgo Bash from Sweden. In the 1990s long-distance travelers extended the weekend party from Thursday through Monday, renting every available lodging facility on American Beach and other resorts on the island.

On the night of the traditional bonfire, Michael's brother Dennis and his wife, Linda, fire up stainless-steel pots three feet deep loaded with delicate morsels from the sea and cooked with the flavors guests know to expect from the chef, Mr. Natural (Dennis's professional name). People still talk about the Poor Man's Stew that Mr. Natural concocted from a fresh-caught sixty-pound grouper, gallons of deep sea scallops, a case of chicken, a bushel of jumbo shrimp, chunks of ham, pods of okra cooked to a pulp, and other mysterious and savory ingredients. Each year he tops the previous year's creations. One year the primary concern was keeping celebrants from getting too close to the long, deep pit on which a succulent fish wrapped in an olive-oil soaked cheesecloth was being grilled in banana leaves over a hundred pounds of white-hot charcoal. Another challenge that year was gathering enough banana leaves—Bash hosts knocked on strangers' doors all over the island asking if they could strip leaves from their banana trees for wrapping the huge fish and lining the giant pit.

Activities during Virgo Bash include dancing, fishing, swimming, games, and midnight kite flying. No one connected with the Royal Family misses it. For the first seven years, it was always scheduled for the third weekend in September. One year, a radio station in Jacksonville got word of the event and announced it the weekend of the Bash, swelling the already large crowd. An enterprising vendor seized the opportunity and sold Virgo Bash t-shirts, a slap in the face of Royal Family members.

Too many self-invited guests have persuaded the planners to vary the date. Invited guests are informed at the appropriate time of the dates and locations of activities during Virgo Bash Week.[5] During the month preceding this event, those not in the know cruise the American Beach area to pick up the word as to the important date. Each year the Bash sets and breaks its own records for dynamic beach party entertaining.

Though the winds of change for the community are as certain as the tides, any season of the year and any day of the week is the right time to be on American Beach.

CHAPTER 20

American Beach Dining Rooms

Aromas of sizzling fried beach whitings and shrimp dinners,
accented with the smell of mustard and
Hot sauce, seep from the boundaries of Duck's Place and
Evans' as adult patrons casually sip on
Soothing refreshments while enjoying hearty conversations
and laughter and listening to the Blues.

RUTH LYNAH WATERS

No story of American Beach would be complete that didn't include recipes from the kitchens and grills of the community's fine home chefs. Each recipe carries with it the story of the home and family where it originated, and I have tested every recipe and recorded every story.

THE END OF THE RAINBOW

Deloris Gilyard, a teacher at Fernandina Beach High School and a long-time resident of American Beach, is sought by businesses, organizations, and individual families the length of this thirteen-mile, 11,600-acre island to cater special events. Her arrangements dazzle the eye as surely as her creations delight the palate. She is as good at baking and decorating cakes as she is with meats and casseroles. Her fruit and vegetable trays empty as fast as her shrimp cocktail trays. When the Gilyards entertain, their guests reflect a compatible mixture of the races, cultures, and classes of people that make up Amelia Island, including lifetime residents and newcomers.

SEAFOOD CASSEROLE

> 1 16-oz. pkg. jumbo pasta shells
> 2 lbs. shrimp
> 2 lbs. scallops
> 2 lbs. lump crabmeat
> 2 onions, 1 red pepper, 1 green pepper, and 4 stalks of celery, all diced
> 12 oz. sharp cheese, shredded
> ½ lb. Monterey Jack cheese, shredded
> ½ cup margarine
> 4 eggs, beaten
> 1½ cups milk
> 1 can cream of chicken soup
> 1 can golden mushroom soup
> 1 lb. frozen English peas
> 1 tbsp. parsley
> 1 tsp. salt
> 1 tsp. black pepper
> 1 tsp. Accent
> Dash of hot sauce
> 2 cups crushed potato chips
> Margarine

Cook pasta shells according to directions. Cook frozen peas according to directions. Saute onions, peppers, and celery. Peel and devein shrimp, drop in boiling water, remove as soon as shrimp turn pink. In large mixing bowl stir in all ingredients except the cheese and potato chips, being careful to keep crabmeat in lumps.

Spray casserole dish with Pam. Put a layer of combined mixture in casserole dish; sprinkle with cheese. Put another layer of combined mixture in dish and finally sprinkle with cheese and potato chips. Dot with margarine. Bake at 325° for one hour.

This recipe feeds as many as can be seated at a dining room and kitchen table, with extra servings left over for the cook. When I gathered all of the ingredients for this recipe and was ready to prepare it, I asked Deloris Gilyard if I could use canned English peas instead of the frozen ones. She said that I could, but she used frozen peas because they maintained the texture and natural color of fresh peas. I went back to the store and bought the frozen peas.

Deloris Gilyard enjoys remembering stories about her grandfather, Lemon Green. In the early 1960s, her father and grandfather caught the bus to go to Jacksonville to buy a used car that they had seen advertised in the newspaper. When the owner saw her grandfather, a Cherokee, and her father, an African American, he decided not to sell. On the way home, her disappointed father and grandfather spotted a truck for sale out the Greyhound window and got off the bus to inquire. This owner was willing to sell to a Cherokee, and they were able to drive the faded red truck home.

When Deloris Gilyard's grandfather retired from his job counting logs at the sawmill, he received his monthly check by mail. The day the check arrived, they had a party. Every month. The party treat always consisted of one item, a bag of corn candy. Grandfather, grandmother, and all the children sat on the floor with their legs crossed under them and passed the bag of corn candy; each would take out one piece, eat it, and pass the bag, to make the party last as long as possible.

Deloris and her two sisters and two brothers spent much time with their grandfather, a man of few words and a heart as big as the sea. Whenever a rainbow appeared, their grandfather would take them to the rainbow's end—and all rainbows seemed to end in a peach orchard, a watermelon patch, or a grape arbor where they could eat their fill.

Cruising away from Company

James and Joyce Robinson came to the island from New York; for nineteen years, they vacationed annually on American Beach and bought a home there in 1973 during the black flight. It wasn't long before their siblings and other relatives from New York and throughout the country took to free time-sharing in their guest house. This constant influx of company keeps them busy in the kitchen and out on the grill, as they entertain their gang year-round with barbecued ribs by the case, plus all the trimmings from greens to chitterlings. The Robinsons' hospitality and culinary pampering extend beyond family. They often share savory treats with neighbors. Each month it appears that the Robinsons are hosting a mini–family reunion. To

Joyce and James Robinson dishing up ribs, 1996. Courtesy James Robinson.

get away from it all, they frequently go on cruises. They never tire of the ocean but need a respite from the demands on their hospitality on American Beach.

The down-home, low-country cooking served from the Robinsons' kitchen and grill is a gastronomic feast that often climaxes with Joyce Robinson's cheesecake glazed with strawberries, blueberries, or cherries. (This is a make-ahead cheesecake. If you spread chopped walnuts on the bottom of the cake pan before adding the cookie dough, it's even more delicious.)

Cheesecake

First make the cookie-dough crust:

1 cup sifted flour
¼ cup sugar
1 lemon rind grated
1 egg yolk
½ cup soft butter

Mix flour and sugar. Add remaining ingredients and mix well. Chill an hour. Butter bottom and sides of springform cheesecake pan. Roll one third of dough to cover bottom of pan. Place crust in bottom of pan. Roll remaining dough in two strips; press onto sides of pan. If strips break, patch and press together with fingers. Bake crust 8 minutes in 400° oven.

Now make the cheesecake:

5 8-oz. pkgs. cream cheese
1¾ cups sugar
3 tbsp. flour
¼ tsp. salt
1 lemon and orange rind, grated
5 eggs
2 egg yolks
¼ cup heavy cream
1 can pie filling (1 lb. 5 oz.), any flavor

Beat cheese until soft. Mix sugar, flour, and salt. Gradually blend into cheese, keeping mixture smooth. Add grated rinds. Add eggs and egg yolks one at a time, beating thoroughly after each. Blend in cream. Pour into pan with cookie dough crust. Bake in hot oven at 475° for 15 minutes. Then reduce heat to 225° and bake for one hour. Turn off heat and leave cake in oven for 15 additional minutes. Remove cake from oven and let stand on cake rack away from drafts until cool. After removing cake from springform pan to cake dish, add your favorite pie filling topping. Chill before serving.

An Archivist's Dream

Camilla Perkins Thompson is the dean of Jacksonville's African American history. She writes a weekly column in the *Jacksonville Free Press* and is the chairperson of the Bethel Baptist Institutional Church archives, where she collects and displays original documents that trace the beginnings of this historic church back to 1838. The D. W. Perkins Bar Association is named in honor of her father, a prominent turn-of-the-century Jacksonville attorney.

Thompson and her sister Lavinia first came to American Beach with their parents, Daniel Webster and Camilla Bolton Perkins, soon after its founding by the Afro-American Life Insurance Company in 1935. In 1973, Camilla and her husband, Capers, purchased the lot on which her home now stands and started trying to get clearance to build. Year after year, the property survey was returned to them for corrections. Finally in 1984, a year after Capers died, the plans were approved. It was not until 1989 that Camilla, with her daughter Muriel Watkins and Muriel's husband, Guy Watkins, completed building the beach home that had been the dream of four generations of her family.

Camilla annually entertains the Entre Nous Bridge Club, whose members' favorite menu and her specialty includes red bass stuffed with crab dressing, shrimp and crab casserole, string beans, squash casserole, petite rolls, coffee, and a dessert of Jell-O topped with ice cream and cake.

AMERICAN BEACH STUFFED RED BASS

6 lb. red bass, whole
2 limes or lemons
1 lb. claw crabmeat
1 cup chicken broth
6-oz. box stuffing mix
1 stick margarine or butter
1 small onion, chopped
1 bell pepper, chopped
2 eggs, well beaten
Salt and pepper to taste

Clean whole fish, removing gills from head. Squeeze juice from one lime on the outside of whole fish; with the second lime squeeze juice inside fish cavity. Lightly season fish with salt and pepper. Brush inside and outside with ½ stick of melted butter. Refrigerate seasoned fish while preparing stuffing. In saucepan, saute onions and bell pepper with ½ stick of margarine. Now add 1 cup of chicken broth and bring to boil. Gently stir in 2 cups of stuffing and well-beaten eggs. Fold claw crabmeat into this mixture. After mixture has been combined, stuff inside cavity of large red bass. Place fish in greased baking dish atop quarter-inch sliced onions or potatoes, which keep fish from sticking to the pan. Bake in 400° oven 45 minutes.

Pigskin Pork Pot

For the last thirty years on the beach, William and Dot Lucas, the sister and brother-in-law of Ben Durham Jr., have catered to the palate of any of their family and friends who drop by their oceanfront home, welcoming with its ocean breezes and a splendid view. Although Dot's sister Gladys and brother-in-law, Clarence Nelson, are not on the beach as frequently as the Lucases, when they are you'll see the huge American flag flying from the eaves, and you'll know there is a fabulous party going on. Entertaining seems to come effortlessly and constantly for members of the Durham clan.

This generous pork pot serves one houseful of Super Bowl viewers. (Warn them not to gnaw or nibble their fingers while eating pig feet.) Prepare this dish the night before serving to remove excess fat.

Super Bowl Pork Pot

4 lbs. small pig ears
5 lbs. hog maws or chitterlings
5 lbs. pig tails (chopped in small pieces by butcher)
5 lbs. pig feet halves (quartered by butcher)
2 onions, chopped
1 bell pepper, chopped
3 tbsp. cornstarch or flour to thicken
3 tbsp. each vinegar, soy sauce, and Worcestershire sauce
Salt and red and black pepper to taste

Cut pig ears and maws or chitterlings into small pieces; add these to the pot along with quartered pig feet and seasonings. Add enough water to cover meat by one inch; bring pot to a boil. Add all other ingredients and cook on low-medium heat until tender, approximately one hour. Put pig tails in a separate pot and add enough water to cover meat by one inch. Bring pig tails to boil for approximately 45 minutes on medium heat. After cooking, combine meats from both pots; add cornstarch or flour to thicken. Set pot aside to allow time for ingredients to cool. Refrigerate entire pot overnight and skim off accumulated fat. On game day, heat and serve over hot rice.

The Secret of Deviled Crabs

Four generations of Metro and Frank U. Smith's family have called American Beach their summer home. Those who have been around the beach for any period of time know about Metro's succulent deviled crabs. After Metro had made the dish the first several times, she was frustrated at not being able to achieve the texture that the recipe's originator, Elizabeth Alvarez, managed. Finally she went to the source, but it was Alvarez's daughter Margie who gave away the secret. "Your crabmeat is too expensive. You need to use the inexpensive claw meat."

Years later when their teenage son Chip (Frank Jr.) was too young to land a job, his dad told him to create his own job based on the needs of supply and demand. Chip decided that he would sell roasted peanuts on Saturday and Sunday at the beach. After two weekends, Chip had sold only enough to cover expenses. Again his dad advised him to study the market. This time Chip asked his mom if she would make deviled crabs for him to sell on the beach. The business did so well that the sidewalk superintendents ran Chip off because he didn't have their approval to hawk the deviled crabs that beachgoers were running up to him to buy. When his dad presented Chip's peddler's license, the superintendents backed off, and Chip sold crabs until he went to Fisk University in Tennessee.

For best and most savory results, use claw crabmeat for this recipe.

Deviled Crabs

1 lb. claw crab meat
1 small onion, chopped
½ bell pepper
1 hot pepper
1 tbsp. Worcestershire sauce
¼ cup mayonnaise
4 eggs, well beaten
1 or 2 tbsp. cracker meal for consistency
Dash of hot sauce
Italian bread crumbs and butter

Saute onions, hot pepper, and bell pepper. In mixing bowl, combine flaked claw crabmeat and sautéed mixture. Stir in four well-beaten eggs. Sprinkle approximately 1 tablespoon of cracker meal over the mixture, and add a second tablespoon of cracker meal if needed to bring mixture to a thicker consistency. Blend in mayonnaise, hot sauce, and Worcestershire. Stuff in individual crab shells. Top with bread crumbs that have been mixed with melted butter. Bake in 425° oven approximately 15 minutes or until brown.

Not Frog's Legs

Lougenia Jackson Harris is a natural cook whose gift for seasoning and creating delicious meals seven days a week has earned her a reputation on the beach for being able to cook anything edible from land or sea. Family and friends look forward to receiving an invitation in August to celebrate the birthday of her husband, James, where she serves large bowls of Frogmore Stew to whet their appetite for the main course—hot crisp whiting straight out of the frying pan.

Frogmore stew is named for the town of Frogmore, South Carolina, where this recipe originated. The recipe serves five or six. You'll need a ten-quart pot and a spoon with holes.

Frogmore Stew

3 lb. medium shrimp
¼ lb. butter
2 lbs. mild Hillshire sausage, cut in small slices
5 ears corn, cut in half
2 lbs. medium new red potatoes, cut in large pieces
1 large onion, diced in large pieces
6 blue crabs, cleaned and broken in half
4 tbsp. Old Bay Seasoning or 1 bag Crab Boil
4 tbsp. salt

Fill pot half full of water. Add butter, salt, Crab Boil or Old Bay, sausage pieces, and onion. Bring to a boil. Add corn, potatoes, and crabs; stir and bring to a boil for 4 minutes. Add shrimp and stir for 4 to 6 minutes, or until shrimp start floating to the top of the water. Turn stove off and let ingredients set for 4 minutes. Place ingredients in a large bowl and serve with hot butter dip or seafood sauce.

A Fine-Cooking Family

Marie Thomas, the daughter of Rosa and Eugene Thomas, was born in Franklin Town. She has cooked all over the island, from Evans's Rendezvous on the beach to the Pirate's Club on Highway A1A at Stewartville, starting out with her Aunt Hattie, who worked at the Sandbar on the bluff up the road in Amelia City making hush puppies. The Sandbar has been operated by the same family since it opened in 1932, and some member of Marie's family has been cooking there since then. While living in Columbus, Georgia, Marie learned to make barbecue sauce, and she went on to create her own, adding chopped cabbage—people preferred the sauce to the ribs. Marie's cooking carried her to resorts along the East Coast long before Amelia Island became a prestigious name, and she has cooked for private families in New York City and Isleboro, Maine. Her family can't get enough of her purlo (also called pilaf or pilau). Throughout the summer, Marie gathers okra from her garden and prepares this recipe.

Okra Purlo

2 cups of chicken broth
½ lb. whole okra
1 cup uncooked rice
2 slices side bacon
1 tsp. salt
1 tsp. Accent (optional)

Fry bacon until golden brown. Remove bacon and drippings from pan. Break bacon into bite-sized pieces. Cut okra in thin slices. In saucepan add 2 cups of chicken broth, rice, salt, Accent, okra, bacon, and 2 tablespoons of bacon dripping. Bring to a boil, simmer and cook for 25 minutes or until rice is done.

A side platter of spicy tomatoes makes a fine accompaniment to Marie's Okra Purlo.

Spicy Tomatoes

4 large beefsteak tomatoes, peeled and sliced
6 scallions, sliced
2 garlic cloves, minced

¼ cup vegetable oil
3 tbsp. red wine vinegar
1 packet Equal or sugar substitute
¼ tsp. oregano
Salt and pepper to taste

Spread tomatoes in a flat baking dish. Mix all other ingredients, shake well, and pour over tomatoes. Cover dish and refrigerate 4 hours before serving.

The Dean's Dishes

Edna Calhoun and American Beach go back quite a way. She was a property owner in the 1940s, and both of her sisters, Thomasina and Frances, worked for the Afro-American Life Insurance Company. Edna was the dean of students for women at Florida A & M University in Tallahassee until the peak of the civil rights movement in the mid 1960s. For the last twenty-five years of her career, she was dean for residence life at Howard University. When she retired to American Beach, she became a source of support for community projects and vice president of American Beach, Inc.

Since she moved back home, Calhoun's kitchen is a treasure trove to her friends across the nation and to her neighbors on American Beach. When islanders receive an invitation to Dean Calhoun's, all other plans become secondary.

For entertaining, the dean more than doubles this crab imperial recipe. Guests plunge the huge serving spoon to the bottom of the deep casserole dish, scoop, and lift out succulent clumps of genuine crab imperial onto their plates.

Edna's Crab Imperial

1 lb. backfin crabmeat
1 cup Pepperidge Farm Herb Stuffing
1 tsp. cayenne pepper
1 cup mayonnaise
1 tsp. Worcestershire sauce
1 tsp. lemon juice
4 hard-boiled eggs, chopped
A little milk

Remove all cartilage from crabmeat. Measure one cup of stuffing. Add milk to stuffing until it comes to the top of the cup (crumbs will absorb milk). Mix with remaining ingredients. Place in 1-quart greased casserole. Sprinkle paprika over top. Bake in 450° oven until bubbly and light brown, 10-15 minutes.

For her popular toasted-pecan hors d'oeuvre, Edna Calhoun uses extra-fancy mammoth pecan halves, which she special orders from Georgia.

TOASTED PECANS

Place pecans in a roasting pan and dot with butter or margarine. Place in 300° oven and toast uncovered for approximately 30 minutes. Stir frequently, making certain that all pecans are coated.

Day-Tripping Feasts

We must give our own story to the world.
CARTER G. WOODSON

Sweet treats, potlucks, fresh vegetable feasts, elaborate beach banquets . . . a lot of American Beach memories pulsate with the delectable odors and flavors of unforgettable food shared with special friends.

NONCOOKS' RECIPES

Two American Beachgoers and hostesses of note, Corrine Brown and Alice Grant, are acclaimed not for their cooking but for the tasty spreads they put on—they are superb planners and organizers of hospitable gatherings. (They are also two of my special mentors for this book.)

Corrine Brown's family vacationed at the Durham's place every summer. Her Big Mama fished off shore in the early mornings and on the bridge at Nassau Sound until dusk. Today Representative Brown (elected U.S. congresswoman from the third district of Florida in 1992) puts on spreads that keep her family, friends, and constituents talking for weeks. She comes from a loving family of experienced southern countrified cooks who always put it together for her.

Election night victory
party for Corrine
Brown, congress-
woman for Florida's
Third District,
Jacksonville, Novem-
ber 3, 1992. Courtesy
Michael Phelts.

Although Corinne Brown cooks as little as possible, she has perfected the
making of candy-coated pecans, a treat that rivals more expensive competi-
tors in the best candy specialty shops. During her annual Christmas visit
on the beach, she brings this microwave masterpiece she's made from nuts
gathered on her lawn.

GLAZED NUTS

 1 cup sugar
 ¼ tsp. grated lemon peel
 ¼ cup orange juice
 2 cups pecan halves

Combine orange juice, lemon peel, and sugar; mix well in a square or rectangular Pyrex or microwave pan. Add nuts, coat well. Cook for 5 minutes on 70% in a microwave oven with a revolving turntable. Stir and cook 5–6 minutes more at same temperature. Remove from microwave and spread on waxed paper to harden. Do not let nuts cluster.

Alice Grant, a former English professor at Howard University and at Florida Community College at Jacksonville, is a relative newcomer to the first coast; she has only vacationed on American Beach for twenty years.

Like her friend Corinne Brown, Grant makes no claim to recognition as a cook, but she too knows where to go for chef d'oeuvres—to her friend and colleague Saramae Richardson. When Grant enrolled in Richardson's gourmet cooking class, she improved her techniques in preparing desserts. Here she shares her favorite beach potluck treat, a recipe from Richardson's *After-Math Cookbook*.

RUM SWEET POTATO PIE

1 pie shell
3 cups mashed sweet potatoes
¼ lb. butter or margarine
1 cup sugar (use only ½ cup sugar if potatoes are sweet)
1 tsp. nutmeg
1 tsp. cinnamon
1 tsp. allspice
½ cup rum
3 whole eggs or ½ cup Egg Beaters
3 eggs, separated (reserve 3 egg whites for meringue)
¼ tsp. cream of tartar
6 tbsp. sugar
1 tsp. pure vanilla flavoring

Beat sweet potatoes and melted butter together. Add sugar; beat again. Add spices; beat again. Add rum; beat again. Add eggs one at a time, beating mixture after each addition. Add 3 egg yolks and beat well. Taste mixture. If mixture is not sweet enough, add ½ cup sugar and beat again. Pour potato mixture into a pie shell and bake 45 to 50 minutes at 350°.

Beat 3 egg whites with cream of tartar. When eggs have peaked, add sugar one tablespoon at a time. Be sure to add sugar to eggs slowly and beat well after each addition. Stop beating to add vanilla flavoring, then beat eggs again to incorporate flavoring. Pile egg whites on sweet potato pie and return to oven for 5 minutes. When meringue is brown (not burned) remove from oven and cool to room temperature.

Life after Math

Saramae Stewart Richardson, daughter of griot Ruth Stewart, has been a part of the American Beach scene from its beginnings, enjoying a half-century of vacations here with her family.

Since the age of eight, she has been cooking, a task she viewed as an important contribution to the well-being of her family. She started out preparing such dishes as scrambled hamburgers because she couldn't determine how her mama turned hamburgers over without breaking them into little pieces. Back then, her rice looked like grits, and her daddy often commented that her gravy would have to be cut with a sharp knife. But she continued to cook for the family, who encouraged her by eating her meals.

In college, Richardson became the Saturday cook for her roommates, preparing one-dish meals on a single-burner hot plate. Her reputation as a master cook preceded her when she went on to teach math at Florida A & M University, Edward Waters College, William Raines High School, and the Florida Community College at Jacksonville. When occasions called for fine cuisine, Saramae Richardson was summoned. After her retirement, she attended the Southeastern Culinary Arts School in St. Augustine, Florida, wrote *The After-Math Cookbook,* and taught courses in gourmet cooking.

These two recipes from her book reflect traditional beach fare from the times she came to American Beach as a little girl with her family and they bought corn and other fresh vegetables by the bushel.

Fried Corn

6 ears fresh corn
2 strips bacon
Optional ingredients:
Salt and pepper to taste
Accent
1 tbsp. butter or margarine

Fry bacon until it renders all of its fat. With a very sharp knife, cut kernels away from the ears. Scrape down the corn to remove the milk from the ears after the kernels are removed. Fry the corn in the bacon fat for about 3 minutes, stirring constantly. Add seasonings.

Fresh Black-Eyed Peas (or White Acre Peas)

3 lbs. black-eyed peas in the shell
1 large smoked turkey wing or ¼ lb. smoked bacon
1 large onion, chopped
1 large pod of garlic, crushed or minced
Optional ingredients:
½ tsp. Accent
½ tsp. salt
3 grinds pepper

Shell peas and put in water (3 lbs. of peas in the shell will yield about 4 cups of shelled peas). With water to cover, put smoked turkey wing or bacon in a pot to boil until tender, about one hour. Drain water from shelled peas and add the peas to the smoked turkey. Add minced garlic and boil for about 45 minutes. Add onions and any other seasoning and boil about 15 minutes longer.

Tailgate Banquets

During the 1970s, a group of friends and I made elaborate plans for Sunday tailgate parties on the American Beach shoreline. We first prepared a list of compatible people, then created delectable menu items to be served. We decided on the linens, china pattern, and size of glassware. No fewer than half a dozen cars would be lined up for these banquets. We feasted on curried goat, or chicken curry, fried chicken, barbecued chicken and spareribs, fried shrimp, boiled shrimp, even smothered shrimp, shrimp salad, and boiled crabs as appetizers.

Each person in the party was responsible for bringing a prepared menu item. Emory and Countess Baskin and Jimmy and St. Frances Daniels were in charge of appetizers. They roasted oysters and clams by the bushel on aluminum garbage can tops, chicken wire, or extra oven racks. We had plenty to drink. We brought tossed salad, potato salad, marinated tomatoes, and cucumber salad—often my responsibility.

Whatever the entree, Shorty Thompson, our main cook, was responsible for preparing it and other side dishes as well. When his cousin Ella Mae was in the party, collard greens and chicken purlo were almost always on the list. Other popular vegetables were okra and tomatoes, summer squash, baked beans, candied sweet potatoes, and corn on the cob roasted in its shucks among hot coals. We never brought a grill to the beach; we just wrapped our food in aluminum foil and popped it on top of the hot coals for roasting.

My favorite picnic food was barbecued pig feet prepared by our main cook. No one ever called him by his given name, Samuel Thompson. He was Shorty, and so was his wife, Almetha, which sometimes caused confusion. My son, Kyle Dean, was about six or seven years old when he distinguished the Thompsons for us by labeling them "He Shorty" and "She Shorty."

He Shorty had been a cook in the navy, where he had served Queen Elizabeth II and Princess Grace of Monaco. Whenever I had a taste for barbecued pig feet, I carried a bag of pig feet and a bottle of catsup to He Shorty's on my way to work. On my way home, I stopped by, and He Shorty had the most beautiful firm and tender red-coated barbecued pig feet lined up row by row in a roasting pan.

He Shorty cooked by ear—in fact he called upon all his senses. His recipes were sharpened by years of cooking experience. Amounts and times were determined by taste, smell, touch, sight. So were the ingredients. When I tried to write down his pig feet recipe, I was at a loss. How much time for boiling—an hour, an hour and a half, two hours? How much mustard is a little, and how much vinegar is enough? I was able to reproduce He Shorty's pig feet only after many, many taste testings.

Here are two recipes for pig feet, the original from He Shorty for those who can get it by the senses and the other one that I time tested and measured. He Shorty did recommend that pig feet in the same pot or pan be grouped as near as possible by size to distribute equally the amount of cooking time.

We cried a sea of tears when He Shorty answered his final muster in the fall of 1989.

He Shorty's Barbecued Pig Feet

Boil pig feet until tender in vinegar and water.

Sauce:

Catsup and mustard, half as much mustard as catsup, chili powder, garlic powder, sugar, hot pepper, and vinegar to thin out. Remove pig feet from boiling pot. Cover each pig foot completely with sauce. Arrange sauce covered pig feet in baking pan, bake for a while. Continue to baste while baking.

He Shorty's Pig Feet Time Tested and Measured

12 pig feet split in half lengthwise and well washed
2 cups of vinegar
2 tbsp. salt
1 tbsp. pepper
Sauce:
1 quart catsup
1 pint mustard
1 tbsp. salt
¼ cup red pepper flakes
2 tbsp. chili powder
1 tbsp. garlic powder
¼ cup sugar
¼ cup vinegar

Place pig feet in boiling pot with 2 cups of vinegar, water to cover; add salt and pepper, bring to full boil, and cook on medium temperature for 2 hours.

After pig feet have been boiled, remove them from pot, coat each pig foot completely in this special barbecue sauce and arrange each individually in roasting pan. Bake one hour in a 300° oven; baste frequently while baking.

CHAPTER 22

Family Cuisine

We had a five-acre garden with things to eat growing in it. . . . Home-cured meat, and all the eggs we wanted.
ZORA NEALE HURSTON

Both my parents were fine cooks. When my daddy, Charles Daniel Rosier Sr., took over the kitchen to make a meal, our entire family was on hand to help, handing him utensils, bringing forth condiments, chopping or supplying necessary ingredients, and ensuring the right spices were at hand. My mama, Eva Cobb Rosier Lamar, who came from a family of outstanding cooks, worked miracles in putting food on the table for us. Daddy was a good provider when he provided, but we essentially got what was left from his paycheck. Many times my mama relied on a sack of flour and fruits and vegetables from the garden to make our meals.

Hog Raising and Fish Bragging

My daddy, Charles Rosier Sr., was born in then rural Fishweir Creek, near the Kent campus of Florida Community College in Jacksonville. Even when he moved to the city and had a family, he maintained a garden in the country where he raised hogs and poultry for the love of it. Autumn was a rewarding time for us, since we had pumpkin pie or pear pie as frequently as we had grits for breakfast. These fruits, which grew wild in the country, were frequently thrown in the feeding trough for the hogs. Daddy dressed out fresh turkey, goose, or duck for our holiday meals and raised the hams that weighed down our family dinner table. Seafood too was a staple in our diet because he loved fishing more than any other recreation.

Every Tuesday and Wednesday, Daddy's days off from work, he went fishing. For him every season was fishing season. He fished all over northeast and central Florida, on the beaches from American Beach and Nassau Sound to the jetties off Talbot Island and Mayport, on Lake George and the many freshwater lakes from Putnam and Alachua to Seminole Counties. Thursday through Saturday, my brothers, Charles and Kenny, and I cleaned freshwater bream and a variety of saltwater fish for Daddy to give away to his friends. We grew quite sick of this chore. Our strategy was to clean so many fish and then throw a few in the garbage can. Kenny was caught at this once and got a good beating for it. That taught us to wrap the throwaways in newspaper first.

I almost got a beating for giving away a two-day catch of fish to my daddy's friend, Clifford Ray. Daddy had told him to come by the house and get some fish. When Mr. Ray saw almost a hundred freshwater bream, he asked, "How many can I have, Marsha?" I was about nine years old and I said, "I don't care, Mr. Ray. You can have all of them as far as I'm concerned." My brothers and I hadn't cleaned the fish yet, so the more Daddy's friend took, the fewer we had to clean. He took just about all of them. When Daddy came home from work that afternoon, he asked if his friend had come by for the fish. Of course he had. Daddy looked down in the freezer and couldn't believe his eyes. The more he talked about it and raged, the madder he got—with his friend. He called him on the phone, and his friend just laughed—he had gotten away clean. Marsha, after all, had given him the fish.

Both Mama and Daddy loved baked fish for Sunday dinner, usually drum caught from deep sea or saltwater fishing that was too big for frying. It was packed with a cornbread stuffing filled with oysters and pecans, placed in the roasting pan, covered in a tomato-based sauce with bell pepper and onion garnishes, wrapped in bacon, and oven baked. The fish was brought to the dining room table on our antique blue-and-white English platter, which sat empty during the week, called into service only for Sunday dinner. Any Sundays that baked fish was served were lackluster days for us children. We detested baked fish, and on some Sundays opted for vegetarian meals. We liked all kinds of fish—freshwater, saltwater, or brackish water—but it had to be fried.

Our favorite fish were the plump white meaty bream that my daddy caught in the freshwater lakes around Hawthorne and Sanford. One summer morning, it was my brother Kenny's turn to fix Daddy's lunch. The huge bream was dressed out in the refrigerator, and all Kenny had to do was fry it. We children knew nothing about fish fillets or fish steaks, and I doubt if my parents did either. Deboning, boning, or filleting had no meaning for us as it related to fish. Our fish were either split down the middle and pan fried whole, stuffed and baked whole, or skinned and put in catfish stew. When the alarm clock went off at 5:30 that morning, Kenny staggered sleepily to the kitchen and fried up the bream, piled the grits cooked the night before in my daddy's tin pan, laid the fish (a large one that covered the whole pan) on top, and wrapped it in aluminum foil. Then Kenny crawled back in bed, and my daddy grabbed his lunch and took off for work.

My daddy was so anxious this day that he could hardly wait for the eleven o'clock lunch break, when he could wow his buddies with the big fish he had caught. With ceremonial deliberation, he unwrapped his lunch and said, "Fellows, this is how you can eat when you carry your money home." Just before he chomped into the enormous bream, his friend Birdsong Sullivan gasped, "Rosier? That fish looks like it ain't been gutted. It's even got scales on it!" Daddy looked down at the full-bellied swollen-headed fish with its scales sticking straight up and popped eyeballs that oozed. Kenny, half asleep, had cooked a fish from the bag we hadn't cleaned. That was the last time Kenny had to fix my daddy's lunch, and he didn't get a beating either. Sometimes our behavior took the wind out of our daddy. When we did the unimaginable, he just grunted and moaned, and said, "Well, I be damned."

Just as Daddy gave away fish, his friends who hunted gave away their prizes; we were often treated to venison and fresh game. Although we had a barbecue pit in the yard, our best barbecue came from the pit Daddy preferred out at the hog pen in the country. Daddy and Uncle Joe's boys (he had nine) dug long and deep holes in the ground where whole sides of pork and beef simmered all through the night, basted with spicy sauce at every turn over the hot wood coals. Daddy died in 1987, and I never learned his

In-ground barbecuing the way my daddy and his brothers did it for the multitudes, ca. 1920. Courtesy Florida State Archives.

recipe for making the barbecue sauce. This marinade sauce, however, is the one I use on any poultry or pork that I cook on the grill.

CHARLES ROSIER'S VINEGAR MARINADE

1 quart vinegar
½ gallon water
Seasonings to be pureed in blender:
2 celery stalks, including tops and bottoms

1 medium-size onion

3 cloves garlic

2 tsp. dry mustard

1 tbsp. Worcestershire sauce

1 tsp. each thyme and oregano

Add enough salt and pepper to season meat to your liking, as you will not season the meat directly because all seasonings will be in the marinade.

Add these seasonings to the vinegar and water, and marinate ribs or chicken three hours before cooking or overnight. While barbecuing, continue to baste meats with a fresh-made batch of this marinade until done.

In My Mama's Kitchen

Mama's family, the Cobbs, were acclaimed for their cakes, pies, pastry, and well-spread tables at which kin, friends, and neighbors always felt welcome. When ingredients were limited by slim leftovers from Daddy's paycheck, Mama got creative with our menus. In our family's backyard we had mulberry and persimmon trees, and the benefit of the Wilkersons' pecan tree, where the branches hung over our side of the fence. We never tired of mulberry pies and cobbler, or fresh mulberries in season. Chilled ripe persimmons were a welcome variation. We were less eager for pecan stuffing or pecan pies, as we three children had to shell the pecans. Pecans were harvested during the fall, so we did a lot of shelling for the holiday baking.

Sometimes Mama yelled at Daddy that the only thing we had to cook was lard, and my daddy would say, "Fry that!" After my mama had enough of fried lard and sending us to the Jacksonville Terminal to pick up daddy's paycheck, she went to college. Daddy provided a housekeeper for us and took on an extra job hauling palmetto fiber on a two-ton truck to make ends meet. Mama graduated from Florida A & M College in Tallahassee in 1952 and got a job as a third-grade teacher at Oakland Elementary School in East Jacksonville. Our life-style changed completely, becoming much more to our liking.

Mama's best dishes, and our favorites, were seafood. My brothers Charles and Kenny and I often walked to the Seafood Center, where we bought a pound can of lump crabmeat for $1.35. This was expensive, considering we could buy a dozen whole crabs for fifty cents. But we were forced to buy crabmeat by the pound in order to have crab cakes, salads, and seafood casseroles, because to pick a pound of crabmeat from boiled crabs was an impossible task—every other lump would go straight into the mouth of the picker. This pound of crabmeat was Mama's reward to us after we had completed all our Saturday chores. The distance from our house to the Seafood Center was two miles one way, and we had to walk—Mama was afraid riding bicycles would distract us from concentrating on the heavy traffic. Today she still delights in serving crab and shrimp casseroles and salads to family and bridge club members.

She also cooks prizewinning vegetable dishes. Whenever I am asked to bring a vegetable for a covered dish occasion, I take a gallon can of pork and beans to my mama, and my dish is in the oven. Friends who know the secret of these great beans bypass me and go directly to mama to spice up their festive table. (Mama makes this recipe using a gallon of baked beans, two twenty-ounce cans of crushed pineapples, one pound of brown sugar, one pound of bacon, cinnamon, allspice, and dried onion. She cooks this by sense, too, rather than by recipe, and each spoonful is perfect.)

Eva Lamar's Luau Beans

2 16-oz. cans baked beans
1 8-oz. can crushed pineapple
½ cup brown sugar
4 slices bacon
1 level tsp. cinnamon
½ tsp. allspice
1 tbsp. chopped dried onion

Fry bacon; remove from pan. Combine all ingredients including bacon grease. Break bacon slices into four pieces each and mix in with all ingredients. Pour all into a two quart casserole dish. Bake in 350° oven for 45 minutes.

Dedicated Chicken and Rice

My husband, Michael, learned short-order cooking skills as a teenager working at Duck's Inn on American Beach. He worked his way through high school and college peeling potatoes, frying fish, and preparing other menu

Shawntrell Brown, daughter of Congresswoman Corrine Brown, in 1993, keeping she and her mother's annual appointment for a dinner of Daddy Charlie's Jamaican Con Pollo with Michael and Marsha Phelts. Courtesy Michael Phelts.

selections during the 1950s and 1960s on the beach. His most vivid memories of the beach are of buying and frying tubs of fish.

Now, thirty years later, as a member of the American Beach community, Mike continues to be called upon to fry fish for our guests and families. Our favorite fish for frying are sea bass and whiting. I will not supply Mike's recipe for frying fish, as its success is more a matter of cooking technique developed with experience. For example, our neighbor, Frances Calhoun, highly acclaimed for her Southern culinary skills, depends on her sense of hearing in frying fish. She knows the precise moment for dropping fish in the deep fryer by hearing the even, bubbly sound that oil makes when it reaches the right temperature. When the fish rises to the top of the pot, it is crisp, golden brown, all in one piece, firm, and succulent. I've been frying fish all my life, and it's been hit-and-miss every time. Sometimes it's perfect, and other times it's just fried.

Mike is called on at least twice a year to put on the big pot for making Daddy Charlie's Jamaican Con Pollo. This dish is a tribute, and it takes a serious commitment to prepare, but the delight of guests makes it worth the effort. Charlie Savage, the grandfather of my former student Juan Savage, dictated this recipe to me in the final month of his life in 1982.

DADDY CHARLIE'S JAMAICAN CON POLLO

    1 fryer, cut up in small pieces
    3 cups Uncle Ben's Rice, unwashed
    1 lb. large shrimp
    1 lb. cubed cooked ham or sausage (or half and half, 1 cup of each)
    1 dozen cleaned boiled blue crabs, split in half
    1 cup each bell pepper, onion, and celery, coarsely chopped
    3 cloves garlic, chopped
    3 bay leaves
    1 tsp. each curry powder, thyme, and oregano flakes
    1 tbsp. salt
    1 tbsp. red pepper flakes
    1 cup black olives, sliced
    1 small pkg. Bijol condiment and Spanish flavorings
    1 small pkg. Sazon condiment for coloring
    6 cups boiling water
    ½ cup olive oil or chicken fat for braising

First, braise seasoned chicken with curry, thyme, oregano, salt, and pepper; set aside in a large heavy pot. Braise bell pepper, onion, celery, garlic, and bay leaves. Set aside in pot with chicken. Braise unwashed rice and set aside in pot. Braise sausage and/or ham, set aside in pot. Braise shrimp and set aside separately from other ingredients.

Now boil the six cups of water and add the package of Bijol and Sazon. Pour this boiled water over all ingredients in the large pot you set aside earlier. The boiled crabs are added at this point; bring pot to a rolling boil, add the shrimp, stir, cover pot, and simmer on lowest heat for 30 minutes. Yields 12 scrumptious servings.

COOKING THROUGH COLLEGE

I suppose one can develop cooking ability by being in the kitchen of serious cooks. For a while, my only child, Kyle Dean, had a job as a cook. As a boy, Kyle started out as the gofer—go to the store for the one forgotten item: pickles, tomato paste, whatever. He also became the peeler of potatoes and chopper of onions. We cooked on our homemade improvised outdoor grill every week, and it was Kyle's job to pull out the bag of charcoal or gather up lighter wood. When the Mexican restaurant Cisco's came to Jacksonville, Kyle was among the first hired as a busboy; before the week was over, he was making pizzas and other entrees. He earned enough money there to restore my old 1972 Volkswagen Bug to drive during his senior year in high school.

With his cooking skills, Kyle worked his way through Santa Monica College in California. While there, he cooked at Cutter's, the Ritz, and other upscale restaurants. Kyle called home every week telling of the big-name stars who came into the restaurant nightly. He even catered a Thanksgiving dinner for Dom DeLuise's family and friends. On catering jobs Kyle's camera went along with his culinary tools; he has an impressive collection of pictures taken with noted Hollywood entertainers.

From all of his messing in the kitchen, Kyle Dean learned to cook to perfection a mean one-pot dish called crab shala. A beachgoer from birth, he catches his own crabs by the tubful. Crab shala is often used as a stomach liner for drinking rotgut or scald.

CRAB SHALA

4 thick slices salt pork bacon
1 cup each chopped onion, celery, and green pepper
1 #303 can or two 17-oz. cans crushed tomatoes
2 12-oz. cans tomato paste along with 4 cans of water
6 ears of corn, cut in thirds
2 lbs. smoked sausage
1 dozen boiled crabs, cleaned and split in halves
2 tbsp. seafood seasoning
1 tbsp. sugar
5 hot pepper pods
2 bay leaves
2 pounds okra
Salt and black pepper to taste

With fork, puncture smoked sausage in several places to allow grease to escape while boiling or frying out sausage. When done, cut sausage in bite-sized servings and set aside. Fry salt pork bacon in Dutch oven;

remove bacon to cool, then break in bite-sized servings or quarter each slice. Use bacon drippings left in Dutch oven to braise onions, celery, and bell pepper. Combine bay leaves, seafood seasoning, sugar, pepper pods, and salt and black pepper to your taste, crushed tomatoes, tomato paste, and four cans of water; stir together getting lumps out of the tomato paste. Bring to a boil and add corn, sliced okra, and sausage.

Low boil for 20 minutes, then add the crabs to the pot and simmer for another 15 minutes; cut the pot off and let sit for another 15 minutes if you can. Serve over white rice or as is.

PERSONAL SEAFOOD FAVORITES

Boiling crabs is easy. When I'm making them just for myself, I fill a five-gallon utility bucket with water straight from the ocean, pour it in a government pot (a pot big enough to feed an army), bring the water to a rolling boil, and pour in two dozen live crabs. I bring the water back to a boil, add a pound or two of shrimp, then cut off the pot. In less than five minutes the shrimp have turned pink and the feast is ready. You may let the crabs remain in cooking water twenty minutes after removing the pot from heat.

When preparing crabs for company, I throw in a few other spices than beachwater. My base stock is brine from dill pickles. I ask for pickle juice from the deli section at the grocery store or anyplace that sells pickles. When my Aunt Pearlie gives me peppers from her garden, I keep them in the jar with the pickle juice.

The main seasonings are salt or rock salt, red pepper, black pepper, pickling spices, seafood seasoning, bay leaves, garlic, lemon juice, pickle juice, and beer. A few decades ago we simply called it a crab boil. Through the years the common crab boil has been referred to as a "low boil" or a "low country boil," and more items were added to the pot. Other optional ingredients include pork neck bones, pig feet, pig ears, hot smoked sausage, corn on the cob, onions, whole white potatoes in skin, and shrimp. All of these ingredients are cooked in one pot, with the pork parts boiled first. If you put everything in at the same time, you've messed up a good pot because some things would overcook, such as crabs, shrimp, and vegetables. I have seen many a good crab ruined by cooking too long—anything over twenty minutes.

A coworker, Barbara Tirohn, shared this shrimp recipe with me, and I've been using it since 1969.

Broiled Shrimp

2 lbs. large shrimp, peeled
¼ cup margarine
½ cup cooking oil
¼ cup chopped scallions
1 tbsp. garlic, chopped
1 tbsp. lemon juice
Salt and pepper to taste

Coat shrimp in this mixture. Broil on cookie sheet. Garnish with chopped parsley-lemon wedges. After removing shrimp, coat French bread with remaining mixture, broil on cookie sheet. Makes six servings.

CHAPTER 23

Storm Clouds

Everything gained must one day be lost.
FREDERICK DOUGLASS HARPER

Not every day on American Beach is filled with sunshine, tailgate parties, and kind neighbors. The community wrestles still with the law enforcement system, succumbs to nature's catastrophes, and struggles to preserve the integrity of the community geographically, culturally, and in spirit.

ANOTHER POLICE SLAUGHTER

For the fourth time in four years, on President's Day, February 21, 1994, county or city police shot and killed a local unarmed African American man. At the beach for the holiday weekend, I heard on the eleven o'clock news that Fernandina Beach police officers had shot a man named Dennis Wilson on Fletcher Avenue. Could this be our Dennis Wilson, whose brother Maxcell lived in the same block with us on American Beach? My friend Dennis Wilson, who gave me large drum fish and all the crabs he hauled in while seining off American Beach? No, no, this happened over on Fletcher Avenue, the white beach community, and besides, Dennis drove a red truck, not the sports car the news photos showed.

"Approaching Storm" from the photo series "American Beach: A Haven in the Time of Storm" by Bob Self, 1991. Courtesy Bob Self.

The next morning, on my way into Jacksonville about seven o'clock to work, I passed Dennis's house on the marsh and saw, besides a number of cars out front, four somber-faced men in the yard in dress clothes rather than work clothes. It was our Dennis. Here we go again, I thought, with the police and another homicide that will be declared justified in the end. When tragedy enters one home in the community, we all realize that none of us are exempt. Dennis could have been a man from any one of our families.

The Fernandina Beach police and Dennis were neither friends nor strangers. Dennis had just won a settlement from a lawsuit he had filed against the city for a wrongful beating he had suffered at the hands of police. The night he was killed, police stopped him for having made an improper left turn on Fletcher Avenue.[1] Rather than allowing them to arrest him, Dennis drove off, and police shot him through the windshield, killing him. There were no weapons in his car. His wife and brothers and sisters say that he feared police were out to kill him.

We cried and mourned again.

As usual, the police were exonerated.

NATURAL CAUSES

The community awoke to a downpour on the morning of Memorial Day, May 30, 1994, unwelcome despite the 150 thirsty cabbage palm trees just planted along Lewis Street. Vendors all the way from New York to New Orleans would be arriving for the Fourth Annual Kuumba Festival by the Sea; African Stilt Dancers were scheduled to perform; thousands of visitors were expected.

By ten o'clock, the drenching rains began to let up, and by midday the Ocean Boulevard festival site was thick with beautiful people of both races and diverse cultures. Few were on the shore. Though warm and sunny, it was not a day to go swimming; the sea was turbulent. As each wave slammed to shore, it churned up the sandy bottom.

As the Kuumba Festival drew to an end and the crowds began to thin out, on the beach, a few children swam and splashed at the shore's edge. Some ventured out to depths to their knees, then inched a little further out, when a riptide snatched them, the bottom currents sweeping their feet from under them. As the riptide pulled them farther out to sea, screams from the shore alerted festival-goers. Several men and women took to the sea; all the would-be rescuers could see were small bobbing heads. A forty-three-year-old wife, mother, and grandmother of five raced in. So did a twenty-three-year-old uncle, a young aunt, and several vendors. More men ran into the sea.

In minutes, as quickly as the riptides had come, they were gone. The sea continued to smash against the shore, soon releasing five bodies—a little boy, the grandmother, another man, a thirty-six-year-old New York vendor, and a young Jacksonville woman. Rescuers swam past bodies floating face down while bringing those they saved ashore. "The tide just took our feet out and we couldn't go in, it just kept pulling us farther out," said an eleven-year-old, with his twelve-year-old sister among the five who were rescued. "I went under the water and this man dove for me. He gave me to another man, who brought me to shore. I thought I was going to die."[2] His rescuer was Thomas Anderson, a forty-four-year-old former lifeguard of Jacksonville and American Beach, who took the boy to his mother's arms and swam back out to bring another woman safely to shore. No lifeguards were on the beach this holiday. There had been none since the county cut them from its 1990 budget to save $100,000.

FRIENDS AND NEIGHBORS

In spite of mourning their lost, holding on to and preserving the life of American Beach itself is proving to be community members' greatest challenge.

In 1972 the Amelia Island Company, developers of the Amelia Island Plantation, became the community's new neighbors when they bought the Franklintown settlement from African American families who had owned the property for more than a hundred years. The company relocated five of the families to new homes in the American Beach area; it had also bought a portion of the Surher Tract.[3] A while later, the company rezoned their residential property in this tract to commercial and built a warehouse right next to the homes of their friends and former neighbors from Franklintown—a buffer that would separate American Beach from their warehouse and maintenance facility was not needed. Our homes and their warehouse are side by side.

It is a different story at the resort. For the first structure the company built on the former Franklintown properties was a security gate and guard station at the entrance of what would become an opulent sanctuary for the moneyed classes, Amelia Island Plantation. These keepaway gates highly offended longtime islanders, black and white. Theirs was the first gated community on the island.

The company soon began construction on the resort itself. To gain entrance to the Plantation today, you must be either a property owner, guest in a private home, or a time-share renter. Cash is disdained for transactions in the resort's bistros, restaurants, boutiques, and specialty shops. To maintain its records and the integrity of its employees, the Plantation issues cards to lodging guests for recording all expenditures; upon checkout the bill is charged to conventional credit cards.[4]

When organizations such as the Amelia Island Company buy into a settlement, they first hire locals as kitchen and landscaping servants. But once the newcomers are established, the locals get squeezed out. The Sea Island Company has done the same on its property on St. Simons and the Sea Islands in Georgia. On Hilton Head and Daufuskie Islands in South Carolina, developers are "stepping" blacks back from the oceanfront and off the islands. The Amelia Island Company, under the name Sea Pines Company, developed the Sea Pines Plantation on Hilton Head Island, South Carolina.

Many aesthetic and scenic pleasures at the Plantation are bought at the expense and to the detriment of the American Beach community. For example, the mechanic and maintenance facility operations take place outside the Amelia Island Plantation's 1,400-acre compound. Their maintenance facility is located just inside the entrance of American Beach. Huge trucks, including eighteen wheelers, daily rumble down beautiful tree-lined Lewis Street, cracking the pavement, rutting the edges of yards, vibrating homes from their foundations, splitting ceilings, destroying mail boxes. Gourmet foods and beverages from around the world arrive daily at the maintenance facility, where they are unloaded and reloaded on smaller service trucks to be taken to the Plantation's dining and entertaining centers. A fleet of service trucks runs back and forth from American Beach to the Plantation's lodges, villas, conference centers, shopping villages, and sports complexes, hauling in goods to guests and property owners around the clock. The trucks return to American Beach filled with dirty laundry, broken furnishings or equipment to be serviced, empty packing crates, and rubbish to be disposed of.

Security vehicles for the Plantation also operate twenty-four hours a day and provide protection to more than two thousand homes and homesites, as they drive through more than fifty different streets and miles of roads within the compound. These vehicles also drive along the Plantation's four-mile oceanfront, but the only vehicular beach access for the Plantation's 1,400 acres is through Lewis Street via American Beach. Although gates and roads were built before the first villa went up, the Plantation did not build a single road access from its property to the beach.

Through the years people from American Beach have talked to representatives at the Plantation, but the destruction continues. The Plantation paid for a feasibility study for American Beach that addresses areas of aesthetic enhancements that American Beach can and should implement. Yet the plan ignores the devastation of American Beach property by the Plantation's service and maintenance facility.

An ancient forest of dunes and dwarf oaks serves as a natural buffer between American Beach and the two resorts that sandwich it, the Ritz-Carlton /Summer Beach to the north and Amelia Island Plantation to the south. Yet the Plantation has installed a six-foot chain-link fence topped with barbed wire that runs only along the American Beach borders—a continuing reminder to American Beach residents not for a moment to forget their place.

If the loss of nearly a hundred acres from the American Beach plat to the Amelia Island Company on April 1, 1995, is any indication of the community's future, it is bleak. This plat was sold for development in the 1980s by the Afro; the Amelia Island Company, the fourth owner, is developing it into a nine-hole golf course with sixty exclusive homes. Already they are calling this tract Plantation Park rather than American Beach. The buffer between Plantation Park homes and those at American Beach will be so skillfully hidden by landscaping that neither community will know they are side by side in the same tract. Yet no buffer exists to camouflage their warehouse operations.

The Plantation's acquisition of the property leaves an American Beach tract of less than 125 acres.

American Beach residents share a portion of blame in the beach's struggle for survival. Internal strife more than anything else threatens the demise of this unique African American island community. Gains and improvements go unmade as we point fingers and make petty claims concerning who cares more or less about preserving the community's cultural inheritance. As exclusive conglomerates inch closer to the American Beach tract, its identity and stature diminish.

Preserving the Beach

No single book can tell the complete story of any community. For each person who has had experienced American Beach, for each of its two hundred residents and property owners, there is a chapter to be written. But I thank God for the chance to try and tell my American Beach story—so you can understand the depth of feeling in our hearts and souls, and why we think it so important that an American Beach for African Americans be preserved for generations to come.

Notes

CHAPTER 1: AN AFRICAN AMERICAN BEACH

1. Jean McCormick, personal interview, September 20, 1994.

2. Duval County Courthouse, *Deed Book* 82.

3. Bob Price, "Beach Railroad Revisited," *Florida Times-Union,* April 10, 1977, B7.

4. Camilla Thompson, "Reflections on Black Jacksonville," *Jacksonville Free Press,* September 12–18, 1991, 3.

5. Barbara Walch, *Frank B. Butler,* 15, 29.

6. Ruth Stewart, personal interview, July 11, 1993.

7. Jack McCormick, personal interview, September 20, 1994.

8. Frank Parker Stockbridge and John Holliday Perry, *So This Is Florida,* 50.

CHAPTER 2: FRANKLIN TOWN

1. Works Projects Administration, Historical Records Survey Division of Professional and Service Projects, *Spanish Land Grants in Florida,* 215.

2. Charlton W. Tebeau and Ruby Leach Carson, *Florida from Indian Trail to Space* Age, 1:96.

3. Florida Works Projects Administration, Writers' Program, *Seeing Fernandina,* 20–21.

4. U.S. Bureau of Pensions, pension application of Gabriel Means.

5. William T. Sherman, "Special Field Order No. 15," *Memoirs,* 250–52.

6. Nassau County Courthouse, *Deed Book N,* 102; *O,* 128.

7. Nassau County Courthouse, *Deed Book P,* 146–47; *R,* 508; *U,* 370–71.

8. Evelyn Jefferson and Rosa Thomas, personal interviews, December 27, 1993.

9. Lillie Means Ray, personal interview, August 7, 1993.

10. Nassau County Courthouse, *Deed Book Y,* 73.

11. Alexander and Willie Stewart, personal interviews, July 23, 1994.

CHAPTER 3: A. L. LEWIS

1. Leedell W. Neyland, *Twelve Black Floridians,* 53–54.

2. Zephaniah Kingsley, will, July 20, 1843.

3. Daniel Schafer, *Anna Kingsley,* 14.

4. Margery Green and Joan Bentley, *The Arlington Story,* 11–14.

5. State of Florida Bureau of Vital Statistics, Mary Lewis, File No. 1661, Certificate of Death, February 23, 1923.

6. National Archives, Jacksonville, Provost Marshal, *Book 2.*

7. Faye L. Glover, "Zephaniah Kingsley," 49.

8. Florida Works Projects Administration, Statewide Rare Books Project, *Duval County Marriage Records,* 155.

9. Bethel Baptist Institutional Church, "History," 18.

10. Afro-American Life Insurance Co., payroll checks, July–August 1926.

11. William H. Lee, "Forty Years Ago," 6.

12. Eartha M. White, *Seventy-fifth Diamond Birthday,* 2.

13. Ruth Stewart, personal interview, July 11, 1993

14. "Jacksonville's First Citizen," *Crisis* (National Association for the Advancement of Colored People) (January 1942): 15.

15. Afro-American Life Insurance Co., payroll checks, January 1936.

16. Duval County Courthouse, *Deed Book 570,* 274

17. William H. Lee, "Forty years Ago," 35.

18. Clement Richardson, "Southern Organizations," 182.

19. Curtis and Marie Taylor, personal interview, September 4, 1995.

20. Elwood Banks, personal interview, August 18, 1994.

CHAPTER 4: A BEACH NAMED AMERICAN

1 Ruth Stewart, personal interview, July 11, 1993.

2. Alexander and Willie Stewart, personal interview, July 23, 1994.

3. Nassau County Courthouse, *Deed Book M,* 258–60.

4. "A Terrible Tragedy: Two Families Made Desolate by One Rash Act," *Florida Mirror,* February 9, 1884.

5. Ibid., B–4, 75–76.

6. Ibid., 85, 493.

7. Ibid., 95, 92.

8. Ibid., 133, 153.

9. Ralph B. Stewart Sr., "History of the Afro-American Life Insurance Company," 6–18.

10. Russell Henderson, personal interview, February 19, 1994.

Chapter 5: Early Homes

1. A. L. Lewis, Checkbook register, 1935

2. Rudolph Lohman Jr., personal interview, July 16, 1994.

3. Nassau County Courthouse, *Deed Book 39,* 289.

4. Ernestine Smith, personal interview, July 15, 1991.

5. Nassau County Courthouse, *Deed Book 91,* 205.

Chapter 6: Miss Martha's Hideaway

1. Rufus Johnson, personal interview, February 28, 1994.

2. Rudolph Williams, personal interview, April 6, 1992.

3. Cecil Williams, personal interview, October 23, 1993.

4. Nassau County Courthouse, *Deed Book 210,* 169–170; Edna Harris, personal interview, August 20, 1993.

Chapter 7: Ocean-Vu-Inn

1. Nassau County Courthouse, *Deed Book 136,* 271.

2. Alonza Davis, personal interview, July 23, 1993.

3. Gwendolyn Bell, personal interview, July 4, 1993.

4. Michael Phelts, personal interview, July 29, 1993.

Chapter 8: A Who's Who of Vacationers and Visitors

1. Saramae Richardson and James Stewart, personal interview, September 18, 1995.

2. Ruth Stewart, personal interview, July 11, 1993.

3. Bernice Griffin, personal interview, October 17, 1993.

4. Barbara Speisman, personal interview, April 19, 1996.

5. Hettie T. Mills, personal interview, April 21, 1996.

6. Ruth Stewart, personal interview, April 22, 1996.

7. William L. (Billy) Moore, personal interview, May 21, 1990.

Chapter 10: Hurricane Dora

1. Tinye Dawkins, personal interview, December 31, 1996.

2. Willie B. Evans, personal interview, September 26, 1995.

3. Nassau County Courthouse, *Deed Book 149,* 96.

4. Mozella Roux, personal interview, July 23, 1993.

CHAPTER 11: GAY POPPERS, BOOMERANGS, AND HIGH FASHION AT THE CROSSROADS

1. Timothy Alberta, personal interview, July 20, 1993.
2. Barbara Edwards, personal interview, July 30, 1994.
3. Pauline Davis, personal interview, July 23, 1993.

CHAPTER 12: EVANS'S RENDEZVOUS

1. Willie B. Evans, personal interview, September 26, 1994.

CHAPTER 13: SHERIFF H. J. YOUNGBLOOD

1. Teresa Burney, "In Nassau, Youngblood Meant the Law," *Florida Times-Union* June 21, 1982: 3B.
2. Jan H. Johannes, Sr., *Yesterday's Reflections, Nassau County, Florida,* 13.
3. Ben Sessions, personal interview, August 9, 1993.
4. Annis Littles, personal interview, August 28, 1993.
5. Willie Stewart, personal interview, July 23, 1994.
6. John J. Coleman, personal interview, July 14, 1994.

CHAPTER 14: LAW, ORDER, AND RACE

1. Charlotte Stewart, personal interview, August 3, 1993.
2. Selma Richardson, personal interview, July 17, 1993.
3. Alonza and Pauline Davis, personal interview, July 23, 1993.
4. Ben Sessions, personal interview, August 9, 1993; Timothy Alberta, personal interview, August 14, 1993.
5. Circuit Court of the Fourth Judicial Circuit of the State of Florida, "A Presentment of the Nassau County Grand Jury," 4.
6. C. T. Smith, personal interview, August 13, 1993.
7. Sarah Bottoms, "McDonald's Injury Felt by Officer," *Fernandina Beach News-Leader,* August 13, 1993, 9A.
8. Sarah Bottoms, "1993/Year in Review," *Fernandina Beach News-Leader,* December 29, 1993, 1A.
9. United States District Court, "United States of America V. Charles E. Mistler," 1–2.

CHAPTER 15: DRIVING ON THE BEACH

1. Eugene Lasserre, personal interview, July 15, 1993.
2. Selma Richardson, personal interview, October 18, 1993.
3. John B. Darby and Earl Harris, personal interview, September 18, 1993.
4. John J. Coleman, personal interview, July 14, 1994.
5. Timothy Alberta, personal interview, July 20, 1993.

Chapter 16: Stewartville at A1A

1. Alexander and Willie Stewart, personal interview, July 23, 1994.
2. Sheila Shepherd, personal interview, July 24, 1994.
3. Nassau County Courthouse, *Deed Book 133*, 65.
4. Alfreda Frederick, personal interview, July 20, 1994.

Chapter 17: The Irony of Civil Rights

1. Nassau County Courthouse, *Deed Book 502*, 68.
2. Nassau County Official Record, *Book 341*, 130.
3. Ibid., *418*, 543; *386*, 169.
4. Ibid., *107*, 141; *458*, 462
5. Ibid., *117, 720*.
6. Ibid., *Book 112*, 625.

Chapter 18: The Beach Rejuvenated

1. Ruth Waters-Mckay, personal interview, June 12, 1991.

Chapter 19: From Winter Shelling to Virgo Bash

1. Earl F. Colborn, *A Guide to the Birds of Amelia Island,* 5.
2. John and Frances Calhoun, personal interview, June 6, 1992.
3. William (Bill) Moore, personal interview, January 28, 1994.
4. Miriam Burney, personal interview, October 20, 1990.
5. Dennis, Linda, Lydia, and Michael Stewart, personal interview, September 24, 1993.

Chapter 23: Storm Clouds

1. Sarah Bottoms, "Police Shoot Yulee Man, Dies at Scene," *Fernandina Beach News-Leader* February 23, 1994: 1A.
2. Derek L. Kinner and Jim Schoettler, "5 Drown in Riptide off American Beach," *The Florida Times-Union,* May 31, 1994, 1A.
3. *Nassau County Official Record Book 112*, 625.
4. Parke Puterbaugh and Alan Bisbort, *Life Is a Beach,* 384.

Bibliography

UNPUBLISHED DOCUMENTS AND SPECIAL PUBLICATIONS

Afro-American Life Insurance Company. Canceled payroll checks, July–August 1926, January 1936.

———. Pension Bureau promotion brochure for reservations at the A. L. Lewis Motel, 1965.

Albert Price III and Zora Neale Hurston, Central Bureau of Vital Statistics. *Marriage Book No. 10.* Nassau County, Fla., June 27, 1939.

Beaches Area Historical Society, Jacksonville Beach. Issue of the *Pablo Beach Breeze,* June 2, 1888.

Duval County Courthouse. *Deed Books.*

Graham, Marion. Personal archives.

Kingsley, Zephaniah. Will. July 20, 1843.

Lewis, A. L. Checkbook register, 1935.

Nassau County Courthouse. *Deed books.*

Nassau County official record books.

National Archives. Jacksonville, Provost Marshal. "List of Names with Remarks." Book 2 (Old Book 186), RG 393, pt. 4, entry 1614.

State of Florida Bureau of Vital Statistics, Mary Lewis, File No. 1661, Certificate of Death. February 23, 1923.

U.S. District Court. Middle District of Florida. "United States of America v. Charles E. Mistler." Case no. 93-73-Cr-J-16, July 30, 1993.

Interviews

Alberta, Timothy, July 20, 1993, August 14, 1993.

Anderson, Abraham Lewis, August 5, 1993.

Banks, Elwood, August 18, 1994.

Bell, Gwendolyn Langley, July 4, 1993.

Burney, Miriam C., October 20, 1990.

Calhoun, John and Frances, June 6, 1992.

Coleman, John J., July 14, 1994.

Darby, John Benjamin, September 18, 1993.

Davis, Alonza and Pauline, July 23, 1993.

Dawkins, Tinye, December 31, 1996.

Edwards, Barbara, July 30, 1994.

Evans, Willie B., September 26, 1994.

Frederick, Alfreda, July 20, 1994.

Griffin, Bernice, October 17, 1993.

Harris, Earl, September 18, 1993

Harris, Edna, August 20, 1993.

Henderson, Russell, February 19, 1994.

Jefferson, Evelyn, December 27, 1993.

Johnson, Rufus, February 28, 1994.

Lamar, Eva C., July 29, 1993.

Lasserre, Eugene E., July 15, 1993.

Littles, Annis, August 28, 1993.

Lohman, Rudolph, July 16, 1994.

McCormick, Jack and Jean, September 20, 1994.

Mills, Hettie T., April 21, 1996.

Moore, William (Bill), January 28, 1994.

Moore, William H. (Billy), May 21, 1990.

Phelts, Michael R., July 29, 1994.

Ray, Lillie Means, August 7, 1993.

Richardson, Saramae Stewart, July 11, 1995, September 18, 1995.

Richardson, Selma T., July 17, 1993, October 18, 1993.

Roux, Mozella, July 23 1993.

Sessions, Ben, August 9, 1993.

Shepherd, Sheila, July 24, 1994.

Smith, Charles T. and Ruth, August 11 and 13, 1993.

Smith, Ernestine, July 15, 1991.

Speisman, Barbara, April 19, 1996.

Stewart, Alexander and Willie, July 23, 1994.

Stewart, Charlotte, August 3, 1993.

Stewart, Dennis, Linda, Lydia, and Michael, September 24, 1993.

Stewart, James, September 18, 1995.

Stewart, Ruth C., July 11, 1993, April 22, 1996.

Taylor, Curtis and Marie, September 4, 1995.

Thomas, Rosa, December 27, 1993.

Thomas, Ruth, April 22, 1996.

Waters-McKay, Ruth Ann, June 12, 1991.

Williams, Cecil, October 23, 1993.

Williams, Rudolph, April 6, 1992.

Wilson, Dwight H., August 17, 1995.

PUBLISHED SOURCES

Akin, Edward N. *Flagler: Rockefeller Partner and Florida Baron.* Gainesville: University Press of Florida, 1992.

Bethel Baptist Institutional Church. "History of Bethel Baptist Institutional Church." *135th Anniversary Book.* Jacksonville: Bethel Baptist Institutional Church.

Bottoms, Sarah. "McDonald's Injury Felt by Officer." *Fernandina Beach News-Leader,* August 11, 1993, 9A.

———. "1993/Year in Review." *Fernandina Beach News-Leader,* December 29, 1993, 1A.

———. "Police Shoot Yulee Man, Dies at Scene." *Fernandina Beach News-Leader,* February 23, 1994, 1A.

Burney, Teresa. "In Nassau, Youngblood Meant the Law." *Florida Times-Union,* June 21, 1982, 3B.

Child, Lydia Maria. *Letter XXIII, July 7, 1842: The Florida Slave Trader and Patriarch. Letters from New York.* 2d edition. New York: C. S. Francis, 1843.

Circuit Court of the Fourth Judicial Circuit of the State of Florida. "A Presentment of the Nassau County Grand Jury Relating to the Nassau County Sheriff's Office and the Death of Charles T. Smith, III." Jacksonville, July 25, 1992.

Colborn, Earl F. Jr. *A Guide to the Birds of Amelia Island.* Fernandina Beach: Peppercorn, 1992.

Corse, Carita Doggett. *The Key to the Golden Isles.* Chapel Hill: University of North Carolina Press, 1931.

Crooks, James B. *Jacksonville after the Fire, 1901–1919.* Gainesville: University Presses of Florida, 1991.

Florida Census Record 1900. John Hurston. Volume 14. E. D. 117. Orange County, Fla.: 1900.

Florida Works Projects Administration, Statewide Rare Books Project. *Duval County Marriage Records, 1879 to 1885.* Vol. 3. Jacksonville, 1940.

Florida Works Projects Administration, Writers' Program. *Seeing Fernandina.* Fernandina: Fernandina News, 1940.

Glover, Faye L. "Zephaniah Kingsley: Nonconformist, Slave Trader, Patriarch." Master's thesis, Atlanta University, 1970.

Green, Margery, and Joan Bentley. *The Arlington Story.* Arlington, Fla.: Arlington Volunteer Fire Department Auxiliary, 1959.

Headquarters Department of the South, Hilton Head, S.C., January 21, 1865, "General Orders, No. 8." *New York Times,* January 29, 1865.

"Jacksonville's First Citizen." *Crisis* (January 1942).

Johannes, Jan H., Sr. *Yesterday's Reflections, Nassau County, Florida.* Callahan: Florida Sun Printing, 1976.

Kinner, Derek L., and Jim Schoetler. "Five Drown in Riptide off American Beach." *Florida Times-Union,* May 31, 1994, 1A.

Lee, William H. "Forty Years Ago." *Fortieth Anniversary, 1901–1941, Afro-American Life Insurance Company.* Jacksonville: Afro-American Life Insurance Company, 1941.

Neyland, Leedell W. *Twelve Black Floridians.* Tallahassee: Florida Agricultural and Mechanical University Foundation, 1970.

Perkins, Harrison. "He Raises Doubts about Vet's Death." *Fernandina Beach News-Leader,* August 12, 1992, 5A.

Puterbaugh, Parke, and Alan Bisbort. *Life Is a Beach.* New York: McGraw-Hill, 1986.

Richardson, Clement. "Southern Organizations." *National Cyclopedia of the Colored Race.* Montgomery, Ala.: National, 1919.

Richardson, Saramae Stewart. *The After-Math Cookbook.* Jacksonville, 1991.

Riley, Dorothy Winbush. *My Soul Looks Back, 'Less I Forget.* New York: HarperCollins, 1993.

Schafer, Daniel. *Anna Kingsley.* St. Augustine: St. Augustine Historical Society, 1994.

Sherman, William T. *Memoirs of General William T. Sherman.* Westport, Conn.: Greenwood, 1957.

Stewart, Ralph B., Sr. "History of the Afro-American Life Insurance Company." *Afro-American Life Insurance Company Golden Anniversary, 1901–1951.* Jacksonville: Afro-American Life Insurance Company, 1951.

Stockbridge, Frank Parker, and John Holliday Perry. *So This Is Florida.* Jacksonville: Perry, 1938.

Tebeau, Charlton W., and Ruby Leach Carson. *Florida from Indian Trail to Space Age.* Vol. 1. Delray Beach: Southern, 1965.

U.S. Bureau of Pensions. Pension application of Gabriel Means. Filed by William Fletcher and Company. Washington, D.C.: U.S. Government Printing Office, 1902.

Walch, Barbara, *Frank B. Butler.* St. Augustine: Rudolph B. Hadley Sr., 1992.

Webb, Wanton S. *Webb's Jacksonville and Consolidated Directory.* Poughkeepsie, N.Y.: Haight, 1886.

White, Eartha M. *Seventy-Fifth Diamond Birthday Observance of the Useful Life of Eartha Mary Magdalene White.* Jacksonville: Brown, 1951.

Works Projects Administration, Historical Records Survey Division of Professional and Service Projects. *Spanish Land Grants in Florida.* Vol. 3. Tallahassee, 1941.

7-14-97

WEST END

BROWSE 975.911 PHELTS
Phelts, Marsha Dean
An American beach for
     African Americans

Atlanta-Fulton Public Library